"Michelle and Linda bring a clear understanding of what drives customer decision making, opening up previously unseen opportunities for growth."

—Doug Fields,
President, VAM Drilling USA, Inc., Vallourec Group

"If there was ever a time for breakthrough insights into what drives customers to act and lead businesses to opportunity, this is it. The powerful tools Helin and Goodman have created with emotional-trigger research have given businesses around the world the strategies they needed to fuel growth, engage customers, and transform their markets in today's rapidly shifting landscape."

—Russ Setzkorn,
Former Communications Executive, Compaq Computers

"Michelle and Linda have done a great job of providing very specific and usable techniques to help any company strengthen its sales efforts. This book really teaches how to get into the head of a prospect and solve their problem, while successfully winning new business."

—David Ferdman,
President, CyrusOne

"The increasingly difficult challenge of creating business value and sustaining growth make the lessons of *Why Customers Really Buy* invaluable. Helin and Goodman's technique for tapping into the emotional triggers that drive sales provide critical information needed to master customer-relationship management and deliver value to customers. An essential primer for every business leader!"

—Connie Lange Merrill, PhD,
Professor, Jones Graduate School of Management,
Rice University, Former Executive with Shell Oil Company

Why Customers Really Buy

Uncovering the Emotional Triggers That Drive Sales

By
LINDA GOODMAN
AND
MICHELLE HELIN

CAREER
PRESS
FRANKLIN LAKES, NJ

WHY CUSTOMERS REALLY BUY
EDITED BY DIANA GHAZZAWI
TYPESET BY MICHAEL FITZGIBBON
Cover design by Rob Johnson/Johnson Design
Printed in the U.S.A. by Book-mart Press

To order this title, please call toll-free 1-800-CAREER-1 (NJ and Canada: 201-848-0310) to order using VISA or MasterCard, or for further information on books from Career Press.

The Career Press, Inc., 3 Tice Road, PO Box 687,
Franklin Lakes, NJ 07417
www.careerpress.com

Library of Congress Cataloging-in-Publication Data
Goodman, Linda
    Why customers really buy : uncovering the emotional triggers that drive sales / by Linda Goodman and Michelle Helin.
        p. cm.
    Includes index.
    ISBN 978-1-60163-041-4 40528274   6/09
        1. Consumer behavior. 2. Marketing—Psychological aspects.
    I. Helin, Michelle. II. Title.

HF5415.32.G66 2009
658.8'342--dc22

                                                            2008031776

Acknowledgments

We've been fortunate that so many people have been an ongoing source of encouragement, support, and guidance throughout the process of writing this book.

It was Beth Ravit, who began as our client and later became our good friend, who first urged us to share our technique of emotional-trigger research. We are grateful for her input and for her steadfast belief that our story should be told.

The contributions of our colleague and dear friend, Ric Wanetik, are too numerous to list. Ric's vision gave the book its shape and direction. His creativity, professional insights, and boundless generosity were invaluable and will always be remembered as a treasured gift. We are profoundly grateful.

Judith Rothman, a longtime friend and respected publishing executive, was a ceaseless champion of our project. We could not have wished for direction from anyone more devoted or more knowledgeable. We deeply appreciate all her help, the doors she opened, and the introduction to John Willig, our wonderful agent.

As our mentor and advocate, we thank John for always believing in us. We know how lucky we are to have him in our corner.

A special recognition to Shirley Dion, Lois Winsen, and Dr. Louise Menlo, who not only shared their friendship, but were professional sounding boards we turned to frequently, and who always helped steer us in the right direction. And to Grady Harrison, whose understanding of the complexities of today's global marketplace made us smarter.

We especially thank our partners at Career Press, for making our first publishing experience such a positive one.

Finally, to our many clients whom we've had the privilege of working with over the years, it is you who made this book possible.

Contents

Part III
Putting Emotional Triggers to Work—Marketing

Part IV
Putting Emotional Triggers to Work—
Customer Relationships

Part V
Integrating Emotional Logic

Introduction

The motivations customers act on are seldom logical, predictable, or even conscious. Instead, their strongest responses stem from one source: emotion. It's a deceptively simple

> Facts and truth really don't have much to do with each other.
> —William Faulkner

reality, one that the business world has resisted, preferring instead to concentrate on quantifiable explanations for customer behavior. But whether customers are consumers or other businesses, all customers are people. And people are emotional beings. Despite any posturing to the contrary, decisions *are* swayed by emotion. When this emotional dynamic is acknowledged, it changes the way organizations must go about understanding their customers. It changes the way companies must make decisions. It changes the search for clarity.

That poses a difficult question. Exactly what *is* the best way to achieve clarity? As we began to consider this question, we came to recognize the connection between the method by which information is acquired and the frequently misleading information that is collected. Typically, studies are one dimensional. They are designed

11

to collect a series of facts. Yet depending on how those facts are compiled, a number of contradictory interpretations are possible. The missing component in the research is insight.

We define insight as the difference between what is technically accurate versus what is real and enlightening. It's the engine that drives the decisions that solve problems. Admittedly, insight has become the fashionable buzz word for research. Articles are written about it. Books are devoted to the topic. Speeches are given on it. Courses on the subject are available at colleges and universities. The term is even incorporated into the title of marketing associates at many companies. But labeling research findings as "insights" doesn't make them so.

Insights are much richer than findings. Findings are straightforward answers, while insights reflect a deeper, more nuanced appreciation of a given issue. They paint a picture of the emotional triggers that drive customer behavior. Insights result from discovering the connection between emotional triggers and subsequent actions.

An emotional trigger is any occurrence, real or imagined, that produces intense feelings. Those feelings become the reason customers act in certain ways or adopt strongly held convictions. When the link between emotional triggers and actions is revealed, it breaks down the barriers that prevent companies from going beyond what their customers say to the far deeper level of what they really mean. Once understood, companies are better positioned to act on what drives customer sales.

That's why we've always been big fans of research. Throughout our careers, it has been an invaluable tool. We used it religiously to acquire statistically accurate measurements, validate data, obtain feedback, or gain a better understanding about a particular subject. We appreciated how different types of research served different purposes, but, sadly, all too often research proved unproductive, because the methodology was at odds with the objective.

Many traditional approaches that measured, rather than informed, were outmoded and counter-productive. This was particularly evident when we sought to dissect complex issues. As executives, we had become comfortable with numeric measurements, but insights are not readily apparent in statistics. And if it's unclear what the numbers mean, it's impossible to determine the right strategic solution. Even conventional qualitative approaches did little more than confirm pre-conceived assumptions. They were designed to answer "How can we sell more of our product or service?" But that was the wrong question. The primary question should have been "What product or service do my customers want or need?"

Once we admitted that factual input could be misleading, we started to explore alternative ways to dissect complex issues. That's when we came to recognize and embrace the importance of emotional triggers and emotional-trigger research. Unlike traditional methodologies, emotional-trigger research is an indirect approach that disarms customers with unexpected and provocative questions, employs insightful listening, and consists of in-depth conversations.

Our search for a more effective way to analyze complex issues began with an evaluation of the quantitative and qualitative techniques we had commissioned in the past. We wanted to figure out how each of the most frequently used traditional methodologies presented obstacles to finding the truth. Some obstacles were obvious, others more subtle. But the very real likelihood of making the wrong decision, unless we uncovered the authentic reasons that explained customer behavior, was a powerful impetus for rethinking data collection methods.

Why Customers Really Buy: Uncovering the Emotional Triggers That Drive Sales shares what we discovered about the power of emotional insights and how we used this knowledge to help transform companies.

Throughout history leaders have relied on information for reaching conclusions and making decisions. Yet, instinctively, they recognized that facts alone were not enough. So they sought to supplement facts with insights. That's why they used any means at their disposal, including personal experiences, collective wisdom, envoys, secondhand reports, documents, even rumors, as a basis for making major transformational decisions.

This balance between quantitative and qualitative methods to acquire knowledge has always existed. More recently, the emergence of sophisticated research techniques, global communications, technology, and the Internet, have all converged to give us greater access to hard facts. With this access, we've shifted our reliance from what must be interpreted to what can be measured. As quantitative information has achieved dominance, it's become the rationalization for actions taken or planned. Facts, quite literally, have become the currency of justification. In the process, qualitative or "emotional data" has often been devalued.

But we believe emotional data is more than a valuable tool; we believe it often makes the critical difference. We believe what is technically accurate may not provide real clarity. So as we strive to learn the truth, it's our intention to bring emotional data out of the closet and give it the rightful place it deserves.

Part I

Discovering the
Power of Emotion

Chapter 1

The Power of Emotion

What Emotional Triggers Are and Why They Matter

If Only!

> When dealing with people, remember you are not dealing with creatures of logic, but creatures of emotion.
> —Dale Carnegie

How many times, when struggling to solve a complex business problem, have you thought how much simpler your life would be if only everything was a matter of black and white? If there were no gray areas? If we lived in a world of absolutes, free of "ifs," "ands," or "buts," where customers said what they meant and meant what they said? If a direct question always led to the one right solution? But the business world we actually inhabit is nothing like that. It's complicated, nuanced, and frequently perplexing. Yet despite mounting evidence to the contrary, many of us steadfastly cling to the belief that complex issues can be solved only if they can be measured. In our search for the truth, we gravitate toward statistically verifiable answers. Such answers give us a sense of security, because they are concrete, unambiguous, and absolute. If only statistically verifiable answers were always the right answers. If only they led to the one right solution. If only!

The Real World

If only, indeed. Repeatedly searching for black and white answers when surrounded by so many shades of gray proved to be a futile exercise. Time and again, it failed to elicit meaningful customer insights. There had to be a better way. Fortunately, we did find a better way: emotional-trigger research. Unlike traditional methodologies, emotional-trigger research is an indirect approach that disarms customers with unexpected and provocative questions. This technique uncovers the core, unfiltered, and spontaneous triggers that drive customer sales.

Emotional-trigger research demonstrates how to go beyond the obvious and capitalize on the unexpected. Classic behavioral research has shown it is nearly impossible for customers to maintain a line of reasoning they don't truly believe for more than 15 or 20 minutes. This is the simple, yet powerful, key to emotional-trigger research. In contrast to other interview techniques, emotional-trigger research relies on unstructured, in-depth, one-on-one exchanges. The length of the conversation, combined with an unexpected and engaging approach, gets beyond customers' predictable answers to the hidden reasons behind their actions.

Specifically, emotional-trigger research pairs provocative open-ended questions with insightful listening, in-depth conversations, and close observation of body language to open a psychological window into your customers' deeply held attitudes and beliefs. The insights they reveal provide the hard edges to vague or distorted answers. These hard edges are the emotional trigger insights that give companies the actionable intelligence they need to solve complex problems.

What Are Emotional Triggers?

But what exactly are emotional triggers? How do you recognize them? What's the best way to draw them out? What makes them so valuable? An emotional trigger is an event that causes a reaction. Some occurrence, real or imagined, sets off a series of intense feelings, and those feelings become the reason behind subsequent actions or strongly held convictions. Because they are neither deliberate nor planned, they defy quantifiable explanations. These triggers reflect our inner selves; they emanate from the sum of our life experiences. As such, they are more profound and a better indicator of behavior than statistics, projections, or objective answers.

Emotional triggers are why advertisers continue to spend millions of dollars each year to convince women that blonds *do* have more fun. They are why so many people victimized by downsizing, outsourcing, or mergers go into business for themselves in an effort to eliminate their fear of loss of control. Or why savvy companies understand it's just good business to invest in such initiatives as green technology or community-based programs that appeal to their customers' deeply held beliefs and values.

Why Emotional Triggers Matter

In business, emotion is frowned upon and considered anathema to making good decisions. It's associated with losing control, being irrational, or being weak, though, in fact, the argument can be made that competitiveness, passion, and zeal of the business world are all powerful emotions. Though the business world has yet to fully recognize it, emotional triggers are important, because they strike at a deep-seated chord. They are what we connect with at a level that goes beyond reasoning, because in our gut it feels right, good, or familiar.

Emotions are catalysts that motivate and engage. We act on them because of an innate belief we will be happier, more fulfilled, smarter, safer, more successful, more respected or, in some way, life will be easier, better, less stressful, or more exciting. At the other extreme, emotional triggers conjure up negative feelings and reactions. Rather than embracing what they represent, we recoil. We want to avoid being hurt, embarrassed, rejected, exploited, upset, censured, belittled, or anything else that might frighten or harm us.

Emotional triggers produce responses based exclusively on feelings. They can't be measured scientifically, which is why they defy methodologies that focus on objective, hard data. The same is true for qualitative approaches, which look for simple answers, as opposed to narratives, which provide deeper insights. It's not easy for customers to accurately put into a few words precisely why they do what they do. First they act. Later, they try to explain their actions. The spin put on behavior after the fact is often part truth, part reinvention, and part wishful thinking. As a result, it's difficult to have confidence in their responses to traditional statistical research. On the other hand, emotional triggers provide crucial insights, precisely because they are unfiltered.

Actions always have meaning; the meaning requires a context. By relying on emotional-trigger research, the limitations of more structured methodologies are circumvented. What emerges is a clearer and more comprehensive picture. Customers are encouraged to speak about their experiences, aspirations, frustrations, or beliefs in open-ended narratives, instead of being asked a series of specific questions. What they choose to share and the way they choose to share it makes it possible to understand who they are and what they value. From these open-ended narratives, emotional triggers become apparent. The ability to put meaning to these narratives is the essential utility of emotional-trigger research.

Listening for Emotional Trigger Clues

Learning how to distinguish mere answers from authentic emotional triggers is the next step. There are definite clues that make it easier to read the signals. Answers are characterized by measured, neutral responses. They tend to be deliberate, factual, and passive. On the other hand, emotional triggers are revealed through spontaneous exchanges that are longer, livelier, or more personal. Answers reflect what people are thinking. Emotional triggers expose what people are feeling.

We've explained what emotional triggers are and why they're important. Equally important is learning how to detect them. The examples in the following chart contrast the differences between answers that are neutral responses and those that reflect actual emotional triggers.

NEUTRAL RESPONSE	EMOTIONAL TRIGGER
Thoughts	Experiences
Reasons	Feelings
Preferences	Needs, Beliefs, Values
Opinions	Patterns of Behavior
Factual Answers	Narratives
Likes and Dislikes	Passions

Using some of the examples in the above chart, let's compare a neutral response to one that suggests an emotional trigger.

NEUTRAL RESPONSE	EMOTIONAL TRIGGER
Thoughts I thought that movie really captured what it was like growing up in the 70s.	**Experiences** That movie took me back to my junior year in a new high school. Everyone had their own cliques. All the unspoken rules about who ate lunch together, where you sat on the bus, which clubs were cool and which ones marked you as an outsider. I relived it all again.
Reason I like this restaurant because it's casual and the food is always good.	**Feeling** Every time I walk in the door of this place, it's like entering a different world. The crowd is lively, everyone seems to be having fun, and, for a few hours, I don't have a care in the world.

Neutral Response	Emotional Trigger
Factual Answer I stopped staying at that hotel because the service wasn't very good.	**Narrative** I've stayed at that hotel at least six times in the past year, and yet the staff never remembers me. Even though I always ask for a room away from the elevator, they don't have my request on file, and half the time it's ignored. When I complain, they apologize. The excuse they offer is that they're totally booked, but I've seen people who check in after me get the room I wanted, and they never offer a reasonable explanation when I complain. Half the time, my room service order is wrong, or it takes so long to arrive that I've fallen asleep. And don't get me started on wake-up calls.
Dislike I've never liked the people next door.	**Passion** If those meddlesome neighbors stick their nose in our business just one more time, I'm going to explode! They have more nerve than anyone I've ever met. I'd rather have my teeth pulled than spend one more minute with them.

Looking for Emotional Trigger Clues

In addition to verbal responses, the body language and general demeanor of the customers being interviewed also offer important emotional-trigger clues. The way they sit, how they move, their manner of speech, and where they look all help to separate answers from emotional triggers. Direct eye contact, modulated voices, relaxed seated positions, and calm behavior are all typical of customers who are providing answers. When they begin to reveal emotional triggers, however, their body language and general demeanor change. This chart provides examples of how to spot negative and positive emotional triggers.

NEGATIVE EMOTIONAL TRIGGERS	POSITIVE EMOTIONAL TRIGGERS
Leans back in chair.	Leans toward the interviewer.
Taps or "steeples" fingers.	Uses animated gestures.
Crosses arms across chest.	Motions toward the listener.
Looks around the room.	Focuses on the other person.
Makes hesitant eye contact.	Makes direct eye contact.
Speaks without enthusiasm.	Speaks with enthusiasm.
Speaks in monotones.	Speaks with voice inflections.

Emotion Versus Logic

More often than not, customers act on emotion, not logic. That's why the best data in the world isn't necessarily indicative of how they'll respond. Each of the following stories demonstrates how genuine insights were revealed when the interviewers went beyond factual but superficial answers to uncover authentic emotional triggers.

Story #1: When Fear Overrides Possibility

In 1997, a venture capitalist was considering launching a Web-based virtual advertising agency. The concept was to create an easy way to deliver high quality, effective communications pieces for companies with budget restrictions and limited staff. Positioned as an efficient turnkey service, everything could be done with the click of a mouse. Organizations with sales in the five to 50 million dollar range were identified as the target market. Emotional-trigger research was conducted to assess the degree of interest among a cross-section of businesses within this category. The interviews, held with employees of these businesses who were responsible for advertising and collateral materials, sought to determine what they thought of this new service and what would motivate them to use it.

At first, the notion of a centralized marketplace for creative services was appealing to these overworked employees. They professed to like the basic idea, the affordability, and the breadth of offerings. There was only one problem: the interviews made it clear the concept would fail. When chatting about the virtual agency in general terms, employees were relaxed. Their body language was neutral. As an abstract concept, everyone thought the idea had merit. But, tellingly, they never expressed personal enthusiasm. Instead, they offered only analytical assessments. It was something interesting to consider; no doubt many companies needed such a service. They were nothing if not encouraging. However, once the discussions progressed from hypothetical to personal, their language and demeanor changed. Speech patterns became hesitant. Individuals crossed their arms tightly across their chest. They looked away. Soon enough, they began to speculate on what could go wrong.

Potential customers asked two types of questions. When the concept was first unveiled, they were polite but noncommittal. What they asked revealed little about what they thought or felt. These were the factual questions of clarification. They inquired about the number of creative resources. They asked about the cost or the different features on the Website. Good manners became a substitute for real interest. On the other hand, the questions that revealed authentic emotional triggers usually began with "what if": What if I don't like the work submitted? What if they don't deliver as promised? What if my company's advertising or sales materials are leaked to our competitors?

These questions went beyond trying to understand the virtual agency concept and got at the real but unspoken concern: What if I risk my job by trying this untested service and it doesn't work out? The emotional triggers were very clear, and they all pointed to a high degree of anxiety. These individuals just weren't comfortable with the Internet. The method of delivery was too new, too radical, and too risky. Making decisions in a virtual world unnerved them. They didn't want to try something that was unproven, because they didn't want to get in trouble or put themselves on the line with their bosses.

Today, virtual advertising agencies proliferate on the Web. The Internet is an accepted way of doing business in almost every imaginable arena. But this is now; back in 1997, the Internet was still several years away from universal acceptance. Only the techies and early adapters appreciated the far reaching potential it represented. These potential customers were not particularly tech savvy nor did they fall into the early adapter category. In fact, they were barely using computers. Logically they supported the need for a virtual advertising agency. Emotionally, it frightened them. It frightened them a lot. Thankfully an excellent idea for a new start-up with a sound business plan was scrapped in time because, although the data said yes, the emotional triggers screamed no!

Recapping Story #1

Factual Reaction to Concept	Positive in abstract terms.
Truthful Reaction to Concept	Negative, unwilling to risk failure.
Emotional Triggers	Fear of the unknown. Fear of personal consequences.

Story #2: The Passionate Need for Validation

An international manufacturer of luxury equipment wanted to understand what motivated men under 40 to buy expensive cars, premium electronics, and other top-of-the-line indulgences. Initially, they chose to focus on men who drove high priced sports cars, because these men were also their target customer. Emotional-trigger research was undertaken to gain insights into what prompted automobile choices among this group.

One interview was especially enlightening because it uncovered a nuance that had previously gone undetected. This interview was conducted with a 33-year-old sales rep for a commercial insurance company who owned a Jaguar. When asked to discuss the car's appeal, he initially began by giving predictable answers: Jaguars were well engineered. The dealer provided great service. He liked the styling. It was comfortable to drive. Everything he said was accurate, but the same could be said for any number of less expensive cars. His answers were reasonable and factual, yet they revealed little about him.

Then he made a casual remark about his childhood. That comment provided an opportunity to break free of his pat answers by transitioning the conversation back to his youth. When the questions became less predictable, he was no longer on familiar turf. So, without standard answers to fall back on, he started to share stories that ultimately revealed authentic emotional triggers. He talked about his older brother; a star athlete and high school class president. Apparently, he spent much of his childhood in his big brother's shadow. Now the tables were turned. His brother punched a time clock for a living but the sales rep drove a Jaguar. Bingo! This was the emotional-trigger jackpot. The appeal of the Jaguar wasn't about status in the usual way. It wasn't about broadcasting a statement to the world. It turned out that status symbols are frequently intended as a more personal message to those who know us best. That was certainly true of this sales rep. He wanted his parents to recognize he had finally bested his brother. The sly, self-satisfied grin on his face spoke volumes. As he leaned forward in a conspiratorial way, it was clear he relished being able to rub his brother's nose in the disparity between their incomes. The emotional trigger went to the core of his self-esteem. His ego was dependent upon earning the respect, approval, and recognition of his family.

As this insight was validated during subsequent emotional-trigger research interviews, the international manufacturer refined one of their strategic positioning statements. They still touted the quality and workmanship of their products, but instead of stopping there, the manufacturer introduced another subliminal message into their sales pitch. The subliminal message suggested that purchasing their equipment was a way to prove rather than announce one's "arrival." Subtle language used to reinforce this point hit customers where they lived. It worked.

Recapping Story #2

Factual Answer	The sales rep bought a Jaguar because he liked the dealer service as well as the car's engineering, safety, and styling.
Truthful Answer	The sales rep bought a Jaguar, because he could afford one and his brother couldn't.
Emotional Trigger	Need for family validation.

Story #3: The Importance of the Human Connection

A national architectural firm specializing in hospitals had earned a reputation as the pioneer of a new holistic approach to design. Within their field, they were the first to put forth the idea that how efficiently a building worked was as important as how it looked. Based on this philosophy, they achieved international fame for a hospital that combined state-of-the-art technological advances with a cozy and welcoming environment. Among their many innovations were handheld computers that connected to the nurse's station, in order to seamlessly update a patient's status and manage drug inventories. Additionally, they installed special monitoring equipment that alerted the medical staff when serious changes in a patient's condition occurred. They dispensed with the standard institutional atmosphere by adding such touches as color to the rooms and chair beds that allowed parents to comfortably spend the night with a sick child.

Other hospital administrators, responsible for the selection process of an architectural firm to oversee the construction of their new hospital, clamored to receive a proposal from this team. With a great sense of pride, the firm's president expressed confidence that their combination of cutting-edge work along with a finely tuned on-time and on-budget process would secure their position as the architects of choice. But more often than not, it didn't work out that way. The majority of plum assignments went elsewhere. As the president grew increasingly concerned, he turned to emotional-trigger research to understand what was happening and why.

Initially, the hospital administrators who were interviewed emphasized it was a very difficult decision. They took great pains to be complimentary about all the design firms that had submitted proposals. In measured and matter-of-fact tones, they went on to explain their decisions were based on some added spark in a particular firm's proposal. Maybe the structure was particularly distinctive, or the approach to technology integration was unique. Everyone had a specific and factual reason for deciding to go with the competition.

When the hospital administrators spoke about their projects, they were filled with passion. As they leaned forward in their chairs, many began lengthy narratives that demonstrated how they yearned to be forward thinkers and how eager they were to align themselves with a firm accustomed to working outside the box. But when they began discussing the architectural firm in question, their body language changed. They shifted in their chairs, gazed out the window, and avoided making eye contact. Some even sighed. In time, they admitted their disappointment and frustration with the presentation. It seemed the president had taken over the entire sales pitch while the team members who would actually be working on the project never said a word. They contributed nothing to the conversation. There was no spontaneity or exchange of ideas. The meeting felt dull and uninspired.

Emotional triggers revealed the selection of an architectural firm was driven as much by personal dynamics as by professional qualifications. It was a given that only qualified firms participated in the review. Hospital administrators were very focused on the team they'd be working with on-site for the next several years. They didn't want to spend that much time with "strangers." So, ultimately, it was the relationship considerations that made the difference.

Yet this team came across as distant; they seemed to view the assignment as just another routine project. The tipping point for hospital administrators wasn't about substantive issues, it was about the lack of a human connection. Above all else, they valued professionals who shared their sense of excitement and demonstrated a commitment to the project. Unfortunately, this stellar architectural firm had failed to recognize the emotional triggers that motivated these potential clients. That was the real reason they had lost so many assignments.

Recapping Story #3

Factual Answer	Another firm submitted a better design or technology solution.
Truthful Answer	They didn't feel personally comfortable with the design team.
Emotional Trigger	Need for a genuine "human" connection.

The Total Picture

The essence of emotional-trigger research is listening and looking for the clues that expose a customer's true feelings. Their stories paint a picture that provides the backdrop. It is through these stories that customers share their experiences, passions, feelings, needs, beliefs, and values. Their general demeanor and specific body language further reinforce the meaning behind their words. Together, these clues reveal the genuine insights necessary to see the total picture.

Chapter 2

Emotional-Trigger Research

Winning Using the Indirect Approach

Emotional-Trigger Research

> Listen and be led.
> —L.M. Heroux

Emotional-trigger research is a powerful tool for separating what is accurate from what is real. Through insightful listening and informed probing, emotional-trigger research makes it possible to go beyond what customers say to hear what they really mean. In the process, genuine insights emerge, and those insights become the basis for converting emotional considerations into strategic solutions.

The Technique

The emotional-trigger research technique utilizes what we call the indirect approach: provocative open-ended questions framed around a particular research objective. Rather than using a prepared discussion guide to solicit answers, interviewers encourage customers to share lengthy narratives that provide insights into their true motivations. By following the thread of the conversation as led by the customer, it inevitably goes to places the interviewer had not foreseen. Digging into issues your organization may not have considered, or may not have considered in the way they were raised, is exactly what makes the process unique and enlightening. That doesn't mean emotional-trigger research isn't focused on clarifying specific issues or assisting organizations solve specific problems. The reason this technique deliberately employs an indirect approach is because we found when customers are relaxed, they give more spontaneous and honest answers. Key words or phrases, inserted into open-ended questions, are used to set the tone and steer the conversation. By using such guideposts, rather than prepared discussion guides, emotional-trigger research addresses your company's objectives, but avoids the pitfalls associated with a structured questionnaire.

The open nature of the conversation encourages customers to share candid feedback in their own words. Key emotional triggers are revealed slowly through the unscripted narratives. Typically, customers respond in ways that make them look good or appear smart. But emotional-trigger research is disarming. Customers are more open, because they become engaged with the provocative open-ended questions. The methodology's indirect approach is unexpected and non-threatening. As a result, those being interviewed become less guarded.

The Benefit

No single factor hampers an organization's ability to successfully achieve its objectives more than "inside out" thinking. Inside out thinking occurs when management relies on internal opinions to decide what their customers want, value, or believe. Too often, subsequent research is designed to simply validate these insular conclusions. Emotional-trigger research brings a fresh perspective. It completely eliminates any inward-looking bias by relying on an unstructured format. Rather than answering questions someone has decided in advance are key issues, customers are free to discuss what they care about most, in their own way. Emotional-trigger research is an "outside in" methodology. Topics or pre-determined questions are not filtered in advance by internal considerations. Instead, the focus is exclusively on the customers you want to influence. By actively listening to what they say, you learn the truth.

The Purpose

Emotional-trigger research assists organizations to determine:

- ▣ What factors influence the decision-making process.
- ▣ What causes specific actions or inspires strongly held convictions.
- ▣ What values and beliefs exist within a particular customer group.
- ▣ How the values and beliefs of a particular customer group connect, or fail to connect, with internally held opinions.

The Format

Emotional-trigger research interviews are characterized by:

- ▣ Provocative open-ended questions.
- ▣ Insightful listening.
- ▣ In-person meetings.
- ▣ One-on-one conversations.
- ▣ Hour-long sessions.

How Emotional-Trigger Research Began

Throughout our careers, we continually encountered the need to dissect complex issues. Although we started from difference places, we both came to the same conclusions and had great success using what we now call emotional-trigger research. Linda's story began at the American Broadcasting Company (ABC), Michelle's at Texas Air. In two very different businesses, this technique was the most effective methodology we found to solve particularly complicated challenges that defied easy answers. Let's start from the beginning.

Linda's Story:
American Broadcasting Company

Sometimes ignorance can be a blessing. Of course, that's only if you're willing to admit it. Well, I had no problem admitting it. For me, doing so turned out to be a blessing, a huge blessing! My thinking wasn't clouded by preconceived notions of what wouldn't work. As a result, I felt free to consider a broad range of new possibilities. And that's exactly what I did. To my delight, it worked out better than I ever imagined. That's how I came to acknowledge the power of emotional-trigger research. Here's what happened.

Several years ago, I moved to the East coast to join the American Broadcasting Company. After working as a marketing director in music distribution, I found myself promoted into a business development position within the radio division. The company owned AM and FM stations in major markets across the country. My mission was to bring in new sources of advertising revenue for any combination of these stations. I wasn't the first person to hold this job. Nor was I the second. Fortunately, I didn't know the history, or I might have run screaming in the opposite direction. For years, one person after another was given the same assignment. It never ended well. Repeated efforts to bring in new business failed. This failure had less to do with the capabilities of my predecessors than with the restrictions placed upon them.

The Way It Was

Almost all commercial radio time was purchased by advertising agencies on behalf of their clients, but every station already had a national sales organization calling on these agencies, and

ABC didn't want to duplicate efforts. To avoid a problem, those in corporate business development were restricted from having any dealings with advertising agencies. As a result, anyone who knew anything about the industry dismissed the mission as futile. I just didn't happen to be one of those people. I had never worked in radio before, nor did I come out of a sales background. On my first day, one of the senior executives took me aside and said my best hope was to try and convince someone in top management I had a brain in my head. He believed it would be my only shot at getting transferred somewhere else in the company after the sales development job predictably failed to work out. And that was all before he even introduced himself! Hardly an auspicious beginning.

That confidence booster left me more than a little rattled. Once I admitted my ignorance, what should I do about it and where should I start? Perhaps meeting with company personnel to learn more about radio and each of their own operations was the obvious way to begin, but my instincts told me otherwise. All the internal cynicism at ABC might be too discouraging and cloud my prospects for success. Obviously, no one had the answer, hence the cynicism. So rather than looking inside for solutions, I chose to go directly to the decision makers. Fresh solutions required going down a different path.

When air time was purchased on the company owned and operated stations, corporations slotted it into their schedules as local media buys. So finding out what was important to these large companies at the local level seemed the logical place to begin. I targeted the president or executive vice president of sales at Fortune 500 companies, whose products were sold through every retail channel, including supermarkets, drug stores, discounters, department stores, or specialty shops. Zeroing in on the people most likely to discuss the big picture was the surest way to break out of the "advertising box."

Taking a Different Path

I requested executives grant me an hour so I could "pick their brain." They were told the purpose of the interview was to help ABC Radio understand what mattered most to them on a local-market basis. They were assured no attempts would be made to sell them anything. Happily, the majority agreed to a meeting. Now came the trickier part. How should I proceed? It boiled down to two options. Either large corporations had to change the way they bought air time to accommodate ABC Radio, or ABC Radio had to approach the business differently in order to accommodate the needs of large corporations.

It didn't take a marketing genius to figure out which scenario had the best chance of success. Nevertheless, ABC Radio, like a great many other companies, repeatedly took an "inside out" perspective. Over and over again, they tried to convince potential advertisers why they should be interested in the network's local radio stations and why they should go around their advertising agency to buy additional commercials. They tried to tempt corporations with special on-air contests, prizes, remote broadcasts, and other conventional promotions. No one was tempted. But rather than taking the time to understand the potential challenges these companies faced, or what they considered their greatest competitive hurdles, ABC just kept rotating the players expected to bring in new sources of revenue.

Everything was about what ABC Radio wanted and what they felt comfortable offering. How could potential advertisers fail to be intrigued! I knew little would be accomplished if the conversation revolved around what I wanted to say, instead of what the potential advertisers wanted to discuss. With that in mind, my original approach to emotional-trigger research began

> **"...little would be accomplished if the conversation revolved around what I wanted to say, instead of what the potential advertisers wanted to discuss."**

to take shape. I decided to base my interviews on a series of open-ended questions. But instead of boilerplate queries such as "tell me about your business," I'd ask provocative open-ended questions intended to strike at hot button issues and encourage the executives to speak in lengthy narratives.

Although the theory wasn't confirmed until after the initial interviews, from the start, I rejected point-blank questions. Putting the burden on these executives to tell me how ABC Radio could persuade them to buy air time directly from the stations was too risky. If such a limited framework for the interview was posed and dismissed, what next?

Even a general discussion about advertising was taboo. One way or the other, the topic would circle back to their advertising agency. What was the point of opening up a Pandora's Box, when I was banned from any contact with these agencies? That's why I made the calculation to focus exclusively on the bigger picture. Specifically, there were three things I wanted to understand. First, what, in their opinion, would lead to increased sales on a local basis? Second, what did they believe was necessary to make that happen? Third, what, if any, obstacles did they perceive? After settling on what I needed to know, I had to nail down the best way to find it out.

Senior management of major companies would resist releasing too many details about their business to a stranger. The interview had to be about digging up emotionally charged responses, rather than factual but superficial ones. From the outset I rejected the idea of developing a discussion guide. Intuitively, it reinforced the impression of a survey, and that wasn't conducive to a relaxed conversation. It just didn't seem the best technique to cultivate a meaningful dialogue. There was also the real danger of basing a prepared discussion guide on what I thought was most relevant. As I've already admitted, I was pretty ignorant about the radio industry. Why should I set myself up as an authority?

Disarm and Engage

Instead of pressing executives for specific answers they'd be reluctant to supply, I chose to skirt sensitive matters by taking an indirect route. Provocative open-ended questions avoided putting respondents on the spot, while hopefully intriguing them at the same time. They'd be free to take the conversation wherever they wanted and in whatever manner they chose. I believed that following the thread of their conversation, interjecting additional open-ended questions and prompts along the way, would eventually provide a nuanced understanding of key issues.

The interviews consisted of a few open-ended questions that had to accomplish three things. First, they had to be thought-provoking. Second, they had to be pertinent to the objective. And finally, they had to be wide-ranging enough to encourage an expansive reply. Each open-ended question had to serve as a natural lead-in to additional open-ended questions and prompts.

Several variations of the first question were tested to see which was most effective. For example, a few variations of one question were:

- Share a story with me about the biggest thorn in your side that's interfering with your plans to increase sales in local markets.

- If you found yourself at a cocktail party sharing "war stories" with other executives about your competitive nightmares in local markets, what single incident would you be most likely to talk about? Why?

- If you were granted only one wish, what is the one thing you'd ask for that would make the biggest difference in your ability to jumpstart your business in local markets? Why?

Then follow-up prompts would be used to encourage executives to elaborate in detail on the first open-ended question before moving on. Each open-ended prompt would drill down further for more specific information. For example, I would encourage them with questions such as:

- How did you come to this conclusion?
- What have you learned?
- How has your thinking on this matter evolved?
- How do you envision the situation changing?

The open format of the interviews proved to be non-threatening and emotionally engaging. It encouraged executives to open up and let deeper, more relevant insights emerge. Using this technique was instrumental in bringing about an innovative solution that never would have occurred to me otherwise. From a few open-ended provocative questions, followed by a series of equally open-ended prompts, the answer practically fell into my lap.

Product Exposure, Not Advertising, Mattered Most

In one way or another, almost every executive I spoke with said product exposure at the store level had the single greatest impact on their sales. Many spoke of frustration with their own sales organizations or with their distributors. New items were flooding the market daily. The competition was intense. It was not only extremely difficult to get more exposure for their merchandise, but they constantly battled just to keep the space they already had. Not a single executive mentioned their advertising or media buys as a major challenge or a top concern. When they did raise the subject, it came up in the context of advertising "clutter." They were concerned that shoppers were beginning to tune everything out. It was for precisely this reason the executives claimed exposure within the store was so critical to their business.

More and more purchase decisions were being delayed until customers were physically in the store, and manufacturers knew the more of their product customers saw at "point-of-sale," the greater impression it made and the more likely they were to buy it. The executives I met with were passionate about this need to "break through" at the store level in order to increase sales. Not only was it crucial to their business, but on a personal level, they wanted the satisfaction of "one-upping" the competition.

The Emotional-Trigger Solution

Recognizing the extent to which the issue of in-store exposure translated into an emotional trigger was the genuine insight I had been after. It led to a fundamental shift from how radio advertising was traditionally sold. The real strategic opportunity was with the sales management of major consumer product companies rather than the elusive advertising budgets. If radio was positioned as a "lever" to gain increased in-store exposure for consumer product companies, everyone would win. That insight became the linchpin of a new strategy. ABC went to Fortune 500 manufacturers and suggested a test, funded by their sales division, in markets in which it owned radio stations. The manufacturer would commit to a schedule of 60-second radio commercials; then ABC would host a meeting for that company's entire sales team responsible for the markets selected. ABC would provide all the materials for their sales associates and explain how to position the program with their retail accounts.

This is how it worked. The manufacturer went to a major retailer and gave them 60-second commercials free of charge on the local ABC radio station. The first 30 seconds would be devoted to the manufacturer's product. Retailers could use the remaining 30 seconds to promote anything else they wanted, as long as it didn't compete with what the manufacturer sold. In exchange for this advertising, the retailer signed an agreement to feature the manufacturer's product on an entire fixture in every one of their stores within the broadcast coverage area of that ABC station for the duration of the promotion.

The first company to participate was a leading pharmaceutical manufacturer that ran the program in New York City. When the results were tabulated, the cost of the six figure radio schedule was a pittance compared with the company's incremental sales.

Soon, others within the radio division were enlisted to begin marketing this concept to the sales departments of potential advertisers. Within a year, new accounts included manufacturers of personal care appliances, automotive aftermarket supplies, cameras, food, and a paperback book publisher. ABC turned this new business development strategy into a corporate sales operation, and I was named General Manager.

Win/Win

This strategy worked because everyone came out ahead. Manufacturers had a cost-effective tool to secure more exposure at store level. ABC Radio had a new lucrative source of revenue. And, because Fortune 500 sales executives cared more about how to get their merchandise displayed than about audience delivery numbers, the cost of the air time was not contingent on ratings.

Emotional-trigger research broke the traditional mold. It allowed executives to express what they cared about, in their own words, and in their own way. Without interrupting the conversational flow through the use of a discussion guide or pre-selected topics, the solution became apparent. This technique imposed a rigorous discipline; it forced the focus to remain on what the executives said. They steered the conversation. It wasn't about getting a list of questions answered that someone had compiled in advance. The point was to create a dialogue that encouraged individuals to share stories and speak in lengthy narratives, all the while mining for emotional triggers and the insights they uncovered.

Focus, Focus, Focus

All research is intended to clarify an issue or help solve a problem. These interviews were no different. Although the open-ended questions were deliberately thought-provoking, they still had to lead somewhere specific. Throughout all the interviews, my priority was to understand what factors interfered with the executives' ability to overcome local market challenges. Every open-ended provocative question was worded with that intent.

The first open-ended question set the tone. In this case, framing the issue as local provided the needed context. It was a flexible way to manage the interview, without controlling the topics that surfaced. Through a series of additional open-ended questions, always worded to include a local market reference, it was possible to keep the framework of the session focused on the strategic objective.

Breaking the Mold

Previously, the radio division at ABC, like most companies, focused on what was comfortable and familiar. They talked about audience delivery numbers and ratings because that was the nature of their business. That's what they knew. But it wasn't helpful in solving the business development challenge. In my case, it was easy to disregard traditional fact-finding methods, because I had no particular comfort level talking about radio advertising metrics. Perhaps if I was more knowledgeable, I would have been less willing to explore a new approach. There might have been a tendency to dismiss emotional-trigger research as too unconventional. But because that wasn't an issue for me, I allowed the discussion to go where the executives wanted. We focused on their interests and their passions. It worked!

Michelle's Story: Texas Air

I've always loved solving the problems that no one else can see. That's probably why I also love mysteries so much. Jessica Fletcher, Columbo, Miss Marple, and all of our favorite detectives in film and fiction have that uncanny ability to arrive at the scene, keep their eyes and ears open and their wits about them, and ask just the right questions, ones that not only tell us "whodunit," but why, and that lead to the great "Aha!"

Now, I'm the first to admit, I'm no Jessica Fletcher. But through the years, after having been called in to solve many a baffling corporate case, I've come to the conclusion that the answer to every business problem lies in the hearts and minds of the customers, employees, and stakeholders you're trying to influence. The trick is to ask enough of the right questions to get them to unlock their passions, their fears, and their hopes and dreams. In other words, the trick is to employ emotional-trigger research.

The First Time Ever

Of course, when I first started using emotional-trigger research, I didn't call it by that name. In fact, it evolved from following my instincts. For me, the first time I used emotional-trigger research to pull all the pieces of the puzzle together was in the early 1980s. I had been recruited by Texas Air Corporation to help Frank Lorenzo's rapidly expanding airline group build a unified sales force, consolidate reservations capabilities and break into the national travel agency market to deliver real advantages for our customers. At the time, Texas Air Corp had acquired both Eastern, a regional carrier, and Continental Airlines.

The Backdrop

As in any good mystery, the setting was an integral part of the story. Deregulation was transforming the industry. Airlines were merging

> **"...it was also a time of 'do or die,' a time when only the smart and nimble would survive."**

and expanding. Related service companies were consolidating. Old ways were dying and new opportunities were opening up. It was a time of tremendous promise. But it was also a time of "do or die," a time when only the smart and nimble would survive.

Prior to deregulation, travel agencies had easy, supportive, interdependent relationships with the airline community. They sold tickets, deducted their commission, and were perceived as the destination experts. But in this new deregulated environment, airlines changed the commission agreement. Instead of a flat fee, commissions were paid on a sliding scale based on volume.

Now agencies had to meet specific dollar goals for each airline and manage their business in a completely unfamiliar way. The rules of the game had changed, and they were unsure if they'd be able to survive.

The emerging powerhouses were the large travel agency groups, such as American Express and Carlson Travel. Airlines depended on their Customer Reservations System (CRS) to increase sales with these key customers. Competition among airlines was fierce. Everyone wanted the mega agencies to use their system. A comprehensive, accurate, and fast CRS was crucial to gaining market share. The CRS, proprietary to each airline, was the computer that stored all the airlines flight data and allowed travel agents to book reservations and manage available inventory.

Conflicts of Interest: Egos and Airlines

Frank Lorenzo, a visionary who clearly saw the opportunities that deregulation brought to the marketplace, moved rapidly to arrange the merger of Eastern and Continental Airlines. Unfortunately, there was no game plan for how to blend these very different companies into one corporate sales culture with a unified marketing force and a world-class CRS.

That's where I came in. As the new head of the national sales team for SystemOne, the name of Texas Air's CRS, my job was to create such an operation. We needed to consolidate our efforts and speak with one voice to our major customers. Because mega agencies accounted for 85 percent of our business, it was crucial that we had a good working relationship with them, but they had their own priorities and concerns. Often the two were in conflict.

From the start, the merger of Eastern and Continental Airlines was contentious. Eastern had a very good working relationship with its travel-agency base. They were known as partners who were flexible and sensitive to their customers' needs. Most of their business came from smaller agencies serving the leisure traveler. Continental, unlike Eastern, served the more lucrative business traveler, but they had a strained relationship with their agency partners. They had just completed a test to determine whether they could sell directly to major corporations and bypass the agency community, a group responsible for 85 percent of their total sales.

Then Texas Air acquired three more airlines, and suddenly things became even more complicated. People Express was based on a culture of inclusion and good will toward all. New York Air was the aggressive "in your face" carrier serving the busy New York/Boston/Washington corridor, and Frontier Airlines, the older more staid company, served the western states.

After this five-way merger, each airline continued to operate with a separate sales team. Little coordination in terms of message or cross-selling of products existed. In fact, the sales people were in competition. Not only did they contradict and disparage one another, but they were confusing and alienating customers. By operating as stand-alone companies, each airline was in imminent danger of eroding their business. The whole point of the merger was to leverage increased revenue opportunities, but the sales teams were actually working at cross purposes and undermining the company's potential growth.

In order for Texas Air to succeed, we needed our fair share of Customer Reservations Systems inside the major travel agencies. But before that could happen, we had to establish strong relationships with our top twenty accounts. The magnitude of my assignment first hit home when I attempted to garner information and cooperation from the five individual airlines. The internal resistance was intense. I quickly realized if the company continued down the current path, there was only catastrophic failure ahead.

One Team, One Voice: A First for the Airline Industry

In this fast-moving environment, there was no time to waste. A decision was made to consolidate the sales teams into one unified group responsible for all five airlines and the CRS. This was an industry first. No airline had ever merged the sales functions for their technology system and airlines sales. Nor had any company that owned and operated multiple independent carriers attempted to combine the separate sales organizations.

In order for this as yet unproven strategy to work, we had to sell the mega agencies on the value of this new structure, and more importantly, on the value of converting a significant portion of their Customer Reservation System to Texas Air's SystemOne. From our perspective, this was crucial, because additional exposure led to additional bookings. But just because it was important to Texas Air, didn't mean the mega agencies shared our priorities. If we were to succeed, our customers had to realize a tangible, value-added benefit.

The Listening Tour

Having put a national sales organization in place, my second challenge was to understand what was needed to re-engage the large, disenfranchised agency community. With a limited amount of historical or competitive intelligence available, I needed a way to tap into our prospects' thinking, so I could develop a strategy to meet our very aggressive goals. I started with the premise that understanding what drives behavior, particularly decision-making at the deepest, most personal levels, would reveal what we needed to do to earn support from this diverse constituent group.

With this objective in mind, I began a series of one-on-one, in-depth conversations with the owners or senior executives of each of our key customers. Setting the stage for the interview, I explained I was new on the job and genuinely interested in their thoughts on the industry and their relationship with my company. I went on to say how much their input was needed so we could implement changes that would benefit us both.

The Questions That Revealed Emotional Triggers

Throughout the interviews, I tried to put individuals at ease and bring out the stories that came from their hearts and their guts. We always started with such open-ended inquires as:

- ☐ Help me understand how your business has changed since deregulation. What about those changes keeps you up at night?
- ☐ How would the ideal vendor-partner relationship make you feel?
- ☐ Tell me the story of how your ideal partner today first earned your trust.

As their narratives continued, I encouraged them to expand on their stories by follow-up prompt such as:

- ☐ Tell me more.
- ☐ How did that make you feel?
- ☐ If you had it do to over, how would you handle that situation differently?

Agency executives revealed several powerful emotional triggers that were key to how Texas Air responded. They were anxious. They didn't know where the industry was going, and they feared a whole new set of business demands. They were angry. They were expected to comply with new policies and procedures, but were left out of the planning process. Instead, changes were dictated in a heavy-handed manner. They were frustrated. Every airline had its own set of new rules and requirements. It was overwhelming and cumbersome to manage. They felt that they had lost their voice. Everything seemed to be about what the airlines wanted, not what could be achieved together. They felt disenfranchised. The friendly camaraderie of the past was gone, replaced by serious financial discussions that felt, at times, both threatening and intimidating.

They related stories about being denied critical services for their clients because of disputes with sales reps, or not being offered preferential incentive programs because of previous personality conflicts. They railed about how Texas Air's sales teams were making matters worse. With all the backbiting, they didn't know who to trust. Instead of being partners, they were forced into the role of referee. It was time consuming and emotionally draining to deal with so many aggressive and quarrelsome sales reps. Each story reinforced my appreciation of an industry in a state of change. Old ways were dying, and a new business model was being forged. We could be partners, or we could be combatants.

Transforming Emotions Into an Action Plan

The provocative, open-ended questions led to critical insights. Mega agencies welcomed a more businesslike relationship, but first they needed a clear understanding of what was ahead. In other words, they wanted a "no-surprise" relationship. As the industry moved more deeply into a deregulated environment, they were concerned that past methods of doing business would no longer be effective. During this period of uncertainty, they needed reassurance that their needs carried equal weight with those of the airlines. They sought a partnership, rather than a distributor relationship in which the airlines held all the power. With so much on their plate, Texas Air's growing cast of bickering sales reps was only adding to their headaches.

The emotional triggers revealed during these interviews resulted in a radical departure from what any airline had done before. Immediately I reorganized the sales force and created an entirely new business model. Mega agencies no longer had to endure a barrage of competing Texas Air sales reps. Instead, each account was assigned one dedicated sales person. Historically, an agency had multiple sales people calling on them to represent different products such as air sales, tours, groups, and conventions. With five different carriers, dealing with Texas Air had become the most unwieldy. Now agencies had only one sales person charged with growing every segment of their customer's business. We developed individual sales plans for each company and gained agreement on how we'd meet those goals, ensuring that our commitment equaled theirs. And we took great care to be both proactive and inclusive.

With only one salesperson focused on an agency's business, relationships improved dramatically. Trust was established, and mutually beneficial programs were initiated. Within a two-year period, sales from the mega agencies had increased by 33 percent and all 20 customers had signed agreements to purchase Texas Air's now fully owned CRS system.

Mysteries Worth Understanding

The experience of interviewing customers in a more personal setting, allowing them to tell their stories and relate their needs in a totally "safe" environment, convinced me that this methodology could be applied to many situations. It would greatly benefit companies that took the time to truly understand the deeply held beliefs and values of their customers, employees, suppliers, and shareholders. I recognized how these insights were the key to building profitable businesses, because I observed firsthand how the depth of those heartfelt emotional triggers influenced behavior. I have since refined this technique and worked with companies all over the world to gain critical insights that have repositioned companies and products, improved customer satisfaction, launched new brands, provided proof of concepts for new products and companies, accelerated customer acquisitions, and facilitated change in management initiatives.

And I still love solving those mysteries that no one can see.

What We Learned

Emotional-trigger research demonstrated that the most successful initiatives occur when you approach an issue from the perspective of the customers you want to influence. This technique, first used at ABC and Texas Air, opened our eyes. We realized it wasn't necessary to rely on a structured survey or discussion guide. Indirect and thought provoking questions were better, because they were disarming and engaging. They resulted in richer conversations that took surprisingly productive turns. The executives we interviewed revealed more about themselves and their motivations than they would have shared had the methodology been more direct. This unstructured approach, subsequently named emotional-trigger research, provided ABC Radio and Texas Air genuine insights they had not previously considered. Those insights helped launch successful business development strategies in two very different industries.

Emotional-trigger research is a journey of discovery. It's about provocative questions, insightful listening, bias-free notions and open-ended discussions. By nature most of us aren't active listeners. We like to be heard more than we like to listen. That's why insightful listening is a skill that must be developed. It's not easy, but it's worth the effort. When mastered, emotional-trigger research offers unparalleled opportunities for innovation. Solutions that may not otherwise have been considered emerge in unexpected ways.

Customers will almost always tell you how to impact their behavior or how to engage them if you know how to listen—really listen.

Chapter 3

Digging for the Truth

What Is Accurate May Not Be Real

Learning the Hard Way

> There's a world of difference between facts and truth. Facts can obscure the truth.
>
> —Maya Angelou

The importance of emotional triggers has been underscored throughout the first two chapters of this book because they are what set emotional trigger research apart from other modes of quantitative and qualitative research. Our epiphany didn't come easily. We learned the hard way after years of trial and error. So, before we embark on a series of detailed case studies that explain how we used emotional trigger research, we will briefly share our journey of discovery with you. We do so in the hope that it will spare you many of the same frustrations and false starts we encountered along the way.

Traditional Quantitative Research

As professionals, we, like so many others, heavily relied on quantitative research as the standard approach to gathering information. It was appealing, because quantitative studies concentrate on measurement. They are designed to assure statistical accuracy

51

among a targeted population, by collecting data from enough people to guarantee the sample size is representative of that population. Findings are always objective, because they're based on numbers. And, earlier in our careers, we had a great deal more confidence that numbers always revealed the truth.

Facts provide a dispassionate form of information. At times, this is precisely what's required. For example, a service business might be in the process of selecting real estate locations. Determining the size of each potential market under consideration, the number and distance away of each competitor, hourly traffic patterns by day, the demographic composition of the community, and population trends in the area all require verifiable data. Such statistics may validate a decision regarding where to open a particular business, but statistics aren't enough to enable that business to thrive, even in the best location. For that, genuine insight is essential.

Organizations undertake research to help them understand what factors influence opinions or how to encourage specific actions. But understanding what customers value and how best to engage them is not about statistics.

Why Not Statistics?

More than statistics are needed to lead the way. It requires a huge leap from the facts that are known to what must be presumed. The leap is too great for most companies to navigate successfully. While trying to bridge the divide, many businesses fail to make a safe landing. Quantitative surveys may be measurable, but they lack a reliable interpretive component, because the premise is flawed. A survey comprised of structured questions with predetermined response options represents someone else's perception of the important issues. It assumes, in advance, the validity of a particular hypothesis. If the assumptions are wrong, or if they are phrased in a way that slants the response, the results may be technically accurate, yet they shed little light on what is real.

Quantitative surveys did prove reliable for acquiring population-based or generalized data, such as where to locate a service business. A statistically accurate sampling was the best predictive tool when there was no ambiguity about what was being measured. It was equally useful when seeking simple straightforward answers from large numbers of people about clearly defined and already understood issues. The methodology worked well for tabulating unbiased, value-free facts. It was not appropriate, however, when the answers required interpretation.

The problem wasn't the methodology; the problem was how we used it. We failed to limit quantitative research to questions requiring only objective, context free answers. Instead, we fell into the trap of developing a false sense of security from relying on statistically accurate findings. Using quantitative research as the basis for making complex multi-dimensional decisions was a poor fit. Knowing the "what" does not determine the "what next."

Surveys

Surveys, the most common form of quantitative research, have built in flexibility. They can be conducted by phone, online, through the mail, or in person. The major variables are cost and speed. Each of the delivery methods feature structured questions and pre-determined response options. Frequently, surveys include a list of choices that are ranked in order of priority or in order of preference. For example, customers may be asked to rank the importance of a number of considerations impacting the shopping experience. The list might include store cleanliness, helpful sales staff, good lighting, neatly displayed merchandise, competitive prices, good selection, and so forth.

Although the ranking would accurately report how customers rated the choices they were given, there's still one little problem. Their actual "hot button" might never have been on the list. The emotional trigger may have been something entirely different. Such discrepancies often reduce surveys to nothing more than interesting exercises. Even if the right choices were included, without benefit of interpretation, it would still require too great a leap to go from what is known to what is presumed.

Sometimes a limited number of open-ended questions are included in the survey. But there is rarely time to draw individuals into a meaningful dialogue. Often, interviewers are untrained. They don't know how to listen for emotional triggers or what to do with them. Follow-up questions become mechanical. Because of the way surveys are tabulated and reported, open-ended questions are presented as statistics. They are shown in the context of how many times or what percentage of participants made a comment falling into any number of broad categories or classifications. All of this combines to provide a mountain of facts but little insight. Clarity and the truth remained elusive.

Part of our careers in corporate America were spent working for major retail chains. This experience included department stores, mass merchandisers, big box category killers, and specialty stores. During that time, we hired more than a dozen firms to conduct various research assignments. Regardless of the specific reason for commissioning a study, understanding what customers considered most important was always a top priority. Guess what? The findings never changed. Every survey reached the same conclusions. Convenience, price, service, and selection, in various combinations, were the things customers valued most. It's difficult to imagine in what shopping universe the responses would have been much different. Yet we, along with our colleagues, pored over the accompanying rankings and statistics as if we'd been handed the Holy Grail.

By the time we were senior marketing officers of major retail chains, this type of information had lost its appeal. For example, one company sold children's brand-name toys, sporting goods, furniture, electronics, and commodity merchandise. The same items were also sold by a number of other national chains, giving customers a wealth of alternatives. A strategy was definitely needed to set this company apart. At one point during a strategic planning session, a survey was requested that would serve as the basis for planning a new, broadcast-advertising campaign. As usual, the results were maddening. For the umpteenth time, we received a colorful and beautifully designed report that highlighted the importance of pricing. But it failed to provide any real insight into what good prices meant.

How do you emotionally engage customers if you don't have a clear understanding of their hot buttons? Repeating, yet again, that price played an important role in the overall shopping equation was hardly news. But receiving a report that dealt with price in such a vague way served no purpose. It was a textbook example of how companies are forced to leap from what they know to what they presume in the absence of real insight. There just wasn't enough information to authorize the advertising agency to go further. What did customers mean by a good price and what was the basis of their opinions?

Did a good price mean the store ran lots of sales? Did it mean they always had the lowest prices on sale merchandise? Did it mean customers may not know the price of every item, but left the store confident they paid less than if they purchased the same items elsewhere? Did it mean customers had their own mental list of the most recognizable or most frequently purchased items, and they wanted the store to always have the lowest prices on those products? Did it mean customers wanted the assurance of low prices every day, rather than waiting for sales? Did it mean customers were susceptible to suggestive in-store tactics, such as drawing attention to an item by having a sign with the price in big numbers to imply a good deal?

Don't Be Led Astray by Accuracy

Until those questions were answered, the company was in the absurd position of possibly being led astray by accurate information. The likelihood of making a mistake was greater than the likelihood of being right, if

"The likelihood of making a mistake was greater than the likelihood of being right...."

they tried to blindly make the leap from what was known to what was assumed. The cost of a major blunder would have included expensive, but unsuccessful, advertising; the failure to meet sales projections with associated higher payroll expenses; and, ultimately, markdowns. Additionally, it would have meant there would be less retail space, and fewer available dollars to stock the stores with new merchandise until the old stock was cleared out.

Surveys: The Laundry List Syndrome

Another drawback of quantitative surveys is what we call "the laundry list syndrome." This particular syndrome occurs when too many people or too many considerations are involved in what should be asked. Invariably it turns into a hodgepodge of questions, many of which serve no purpose. The answers may be interesting, but they're not necessarily actionable.

We still smile when we recall Linda's experience as a board member of a regional ballet company. At the time she became involved, the company was facing a revenue decline. Attendance was down from previous seasons, so the organization decided to survey past attendees and subscription holders, going back three years. Given her field of expertise, the board requested she assist the marketing team with the questionnaire design and implementation.

The proposed survey was the very definition of the laundry list syndrome. Every conceivable question was included. The one that still stands out involved babysitters. Previous attendees were asked if they had stopped coming to the ballet because they were having difficulty finding babysitters. If the answer was yes, did the marketing department intend to find babysitters for everyone? If not, what was the purpose of asking the question? It appeared the only reason was to leave no stone unturned, regardless of how irrelevant or, equally likely, to explain away a problem. Attendance wasn't down at every cultural event in town. Surely the majority of other audiences also included a large number of parents. That's why facts can be dangerous; they can hide the true reasons. The ballet company needed more than answers. They needed genuine insight.

Whether surveys are taken online, in person, by phone, or through the mail, it's frequently impossible to decode what the answers mean. Individuals taking

"The truth remains elusive as long as the methodology is at odds with the objective."

the survey may have interpreted a question differently than your organization intended. Then what? Or, they may have dutifully selected from among the multiple choice options presented, even when other considerations were more important to them. Open-ended questions, without benefit of follow-up discussion and clarification, are reduced to over simplified statistics. Bottom line, surveys provide no context for issues that demand it. Quantitative studies are about counting and measuring. They aren't about analyzing and interpreting what people say. The truth remains elusive as long as the methodology is at odds with the objective.

Below are examples of when we found quantitative research helpful and when it was inconsistent with the objective.

USE QUANTITATIVE RESEARCH WHEN:

- ▣ You want a statistically accurate count.
- ▣ You want to validate objective data; there is no ambiguity about what is being measured.
- ▣ You have already identified an issue and want to determine the magnitude of that issue.
- ▣ You want to compare benchmarks.

DO NOT USE QUANTITATIVE RESEARCH WHEN:

- ☐ You have no existing research on a multi-faceted topic.
- ☐ You need to be certain you are exploring the correct issues.
- ☐ You need to dissect and clarify complex issues.
- ☐ You need to probe in-depth for hidden reasons and motivations to gain nuanced insights.

Traditional Qualitative Research: Focus Groups

Qualitative research is more compatible with the ability to explore opinions, motivations, actions, and feelings. For a long time, the accepted wisdom was that focus groups were the best way to tap into patterns of thought and behavior. Focus groups typically bring together eight to 10 people who match the characteristics of a particular target population. They discuss a topic for approximately 90 minutes to two hours, under the direction of a trained moderator. Depending upon the circumstances, participants may be told who is sponsoring the research, or it may be kept secret to avoid a pre-existing bias.

Unlike a quantitative survey, focus groups provide the opportunity to personally observe what participants do and say. It's possible to study their body language and hear their words in the person's own voice. Sounds good. If only focus groups were more reliable. They certainly weren't always reliable for a mass merchandising division of Federated Department Stores, now known as Macy's. This division was a multi-billion-dollar company within this leading national retail corporation. The discount chain generated between 35 and 40 percent of their sales from women's, men's, and children's apparel. But despite how much of the company's sales came from apparel, a pattern began to emerge. The women identified as customers who took part in focus group sessions denied purchasing clothing from the store. They didn't want to admit they bought apparel from a discount chain, because they were embarrassed. They were simply not inclined to be frank in front of other people. Perhaps it was pride, perhaps a form of peer pressure. Whatever the reason, the bottom line was that they were not responding honestly.

When the moderator was instructed to probe further by asking a series of specific questions, most women finally conceded they had, in fact, made *some* apparel purchases in the past. Their candor hinged on whether they were able to position themselves as smart shoppers or whether they felt such a confession was an awkward statement about their social status. Admissions were made in dribs and drabs. Little was volunteered. Information was provided only in response to the moderator's direct questions.

Eventually, most agreed they had indeed purchased clothing for their children at the store. After all, kids outgrow their things faster than they wear them out. It doesn't make sense to buy expensive outfits. And yes, they had purchased brand name underwear for their husbands. Why not? It was exactly the same as merchandise sold elsewhere at higher prices. Okay, maybe if they were already in the store, they might have picked up some pantyhose or a pair of jeans to wear around the house.

What a reluctant crowd of truth tellers! Because the percentage of apparel sold by the company was a readily accessible piece of information, it was easy to recognize when focus group participants were being dishonest. But without such a barometer, how would it be possible to separate what these women said from what they actually did, or what they really believed? Obviously, it wasn't possible.

The Laboratory Setting Syndrome

Then there's the added dilemma of what we refer to as "the laboratory setting syndrome." Perhaps a company has a new product in development, or is trying to decide between several different advertising campaigns, or is exploring the possibility of launching a new service. While everything is still in the planning stage, focus groups may be held to obtain customer feedback.

What could be better than a group of people devoting a couple of hours to thinking about nothing other than your company's question? Well, that's precisely the problem. In the real world, no one will ever reflect on a question being posed in such a vacuum. Instead of hours, they will devote minutes, perhaps only seconds, to making a snap decision. Often their reasons for doing so will have nothing to do with what they said in the focus group. Author Malcolm Gladwell echoed recognition of this dilemma when he wrote, "Asking someone to explain their behavior and intent is not only a psychological impossibility, but it biases them in favor of the conservative, in favor of the known over the unknown."

Focus groups participants are paid to participate. They feel obligated to join in the discussion. But their contribution may have little to do with how they'd react at home or work, when they're in the middle of their usual daily distractions. They may simply feel compelled to fill the void, when paid to think about something for several hours without interruption.

Years ago, an advertising agency scheduled a series of focus groups to test reactions to three different television commercials before finalizing the direction of a marketing campaign. Rather than going to the expense of producing the actual commercials, the agency presented the creative options on large white storyboards. Each frame of the commercial was shown as an illustration, along with the dialogue that pertained to that visual. After the commercial was presented frame by frame, a series of questions was asked.

Did the participants get the same message from the storyboards as the one the agency wanted to communicate? Was the message important to the group personally, and why? Was the commercial likeable? And, assuming the message was considered relevant, was it viewed as credible coming from the advertiser doing the testing?

On the surface, these seem perfectly reasonable and intelligent goals. But years of experience with successful campaigns that increased sales and garnered creative awards suggested otherwise.

Using focus groups to test commercials is fine as a means of screening out what audiences find offensive. They work well as a filter for what to avoid. But focus groups rarely provide adequate insight into what might be effective. One explanation is the methodology itself.

It's difficult for most people to make the creative leap from static illustrations to an actual commercial. They try to imagine what the finished product will be like, but there is no way to know what they're visualizing. Without a way to verify that the audience and the advertiser share the same creative vision, there is little basis for making a decision.

During this focus group, we established that the message was understood. But when it came to obtaining feedback on the storyboards, participant response was entertaining, but not helpful. One of the storyboards featured tokens positioned around a game board. The most vocal participant declared the tokens appeared demonic looking and soon persuaded others a devil was in their midst. A negative reaction to the storyboard ensued, based upon a dislike of the graphics.

Was the feedback regarding the token's resemblance to the devil more than a statement of fact? Was it revealing a deeper emotional trigger that represented a genuine insight? If so, what was it? Was it just one persuasive person's opinion being repeated by more impressionable participants? Or, were participants judging the advertising as though they were advertising experts, rather than the intended audience? And, if that was the case, what bearing should their feedback have on the decisions? It was confusing.

The decision was made to disregard the creative input and proceed with the "demonic" commercial. It turned out to be the right decision. The television advertising increased sales 15 percent, and the agency won a prestigious award. Fortunately, everyone grasped the limitations of focus groups. If an obvious pitfall inherent in the methodology was ignored, the commercial might have been rejected, and the company would have forfeited significant sales growth.

Peer Pressure

The importance of peer pressure can't be overstated. The dynamics of focus groups influence what opinions those in attendance are willing to express or what they will share about themselves. In the case of the toy commercial, one dominant personality took charge. She was adamant the token resembled the devil, and therefore it was bad. Through the sheer force of her will, she enlisted others to share her opinion. Even if they didn't agree, they didn't feel comfortable challenging her in that type of public forum.

Women and Peer Pressure

Women in the discount chain focus groups refused to speak up for different reasons. They didn't want to suggest they couldn't afford to shop at department or specialty stores. They weren't concerned about telling a lie. It didn't matter that they were being paid to be honest. If the choice was between keeping up appearances or revealing the "confessions of a discount shopper," keeping up appearances won out every time.

Men and Peer Pressure

Men are no less immune to peer pressure. A case in point was the time several male focus groups were scheduled for this same discount chain. The objective was to gain a better understanding of how men shopped, what would tempt them to stay in the stores longer, and how to encourage them to buy more. One session began promisingly enough. The mood was upbeat; the group was jovial. They were happily digging into a hearty dinner buffet. Everyone seemed ready to participate in the conversation. A few men even started to discuss their shopping habits.

Then everything changed. One of the participants, full of swagger, declared, "Men don't shop. They buy!" and sneered at the entire premise of the session. Everyone laughed, but, in that moment, the atmosphere within the room shifted a hundred and eighty degrees. The group was suddenly self-conscious about discussing the subject. They felt silly. After the ringleader's remark, the others tailored their responses to what seemed acceptable, rather than what was true. Candor was replaced by humor. Silence or hesitancy to voice disagreement with the ringleader is often mistaken for group consensus. It leads to a distorted perception of what the other participants think.

A November 2005 *Business Week* article entitled "Shoot the Focus Group," provided another illustration of "macho dynamics" at work. It related an America Online experience in 2003, when the company observed a disconnect between what men were willing to reveal in focus groups and the complaints about spam the company received via e-mail. In turned out that when men were in a room with other men they refused to admit they didn't have full command of their laptops.

Business Owners and Peer Pressure

Nor is peer pressure limited to consumers. At the request of one client, day-long sessions were held with business owners of small to mid-size companies. The objective was to gain insight into how they selected their suppliers, what they expected of those suppliers, and, finally, what it would take to shift allegiances.

The input was thoughtful and addressed a wide range of subjects. They focused on credit terms. They discussed the ease of doing business. They talked about the percentage of in-stock at the warehouse. They stressed delivery times. In total they cited eight key operational considerations. The client went on to carry out many of the recommendations emphasized by the participants. But making those changes didn't increase their business.

Why? Because no one wanted to say the emperor had no clothes. Instead of telling the truth and openly airing their reservations about the company's ability to deliver on their promises, everyone chose to take the easy way out. They manufactured reasonable and socially acceptable answers. What they said was accurate, but it wasn't sincere or helpful.

Once again, peer pressure, combined with the laboratory setting syndrome, had taken effect. The group, focusing on nothing else for hours at a stretch and eager to make a contribution, felt obligated to come up with improvements the client needed to implement. They may have reached intellectual agreement, but genuine insight into their true emotional triggers was missing. The hidden reason of why it was difficult to increase sales was because, deep down, the business owners didn't believe the client had sufficient resources or the caliber of personnel necessary to honor their commitments. Each of the participants admitted to this privately, but no one was forthcoming in the focus group.

Instead, they unintentionally sabotaged the sessions. They wanted to be helpful without making derogatory remarks. The business owners didn't know one another. They were apprehensive; perhaps someone in attendance might repeat what they said. So they ended up spending hours constructing a road map to nowhere. They gave answers that made sense on paper, but never touched on the emotional triggers that would actually have changed their behavior.

The Illusion of Time

Other concerns with focus groups began to surface. Although they're billed as a way to explore an issue at length, the math

"In the end, the feedback is disproportionately reflective of the dominant personalities."

doesn't support the claim. Assume 10 people meet for 90 minutes, and, during that time, they are asked three questions. That equates to three minutes per person per question, very little time by any measure. It gets worse. All members don't participate equally, and some, intimidated by peer pressure, never express their true beliefs or reveal their actual behavior. In the end, the feedback is disproportionately reflective of the dominant personalities.

Online Focus Groups

Online focus groups were even more problematic for us. When first introduced, they seemed enticing, because they provided a high-tech means of uniting participants from multiple locations. Everyone logged onto the Internet via a chat room, and they were all connected with a remote moderator. The moderator typed in questions, and the participants typed back their answers. It was quick. It was low cost. It provided a geographically diverse group of participants. There was only one glitch: it didn't work. Unfortunately, the value of the findings was limited. Without the ability to make eye contact, observe body language, or directly interact, it was debatable whether candor could be accurately assessed or responses interpreted appropriately. Consumer-product companies were further hampered by the moderator's inability to demonstrate products or distribute samples. And, because written responses were briefer than verbal ones, an inevitable editing process occurred throughout the session. Participants with limited writing skills submitted less complete and articulate replies than if their feedback had been verbal. Online focus groups turned out to be a hybrid methodology, perhaps best described as a collective survey consisting of open-ended questions.

Deciding When to Use Focus Groups

Under certain circumstances, focus groups are appropriate. As with quantitative research, the problem wasn't with the methodology, but how we used it. The value of the sessions depended entirely on the goal of the research. At times focus groups were useful; at other times they were a poor choice for accomplishing our objectives. Here are examples of when we found the format helpful and when it was ineffective.

Use Focus Groups When:

- ▣ You want practical suggestions on tactical issues, such as how to cut costs or improve a routine system or procedure.
- ▣ You want to distribute samples or demonstrate a product and obtain immediate feedback.
- ▣ You want to use the focus group as a creative brainstorming or ideation session.

Do Not Use Focus Groups When:

- ▣ You need to understand complex issues.
- ▣ You need to explore individual values and beliefs.
- ▣ You need to learn what influences specific actions in an atmosphere free from peer pressure.
- ▣ You need sensitive information that is not conducive to a group discussion.

Traditional Qualitative Research: In-Depth Interviews

As our skepticism regarding the value of focus groups grew, limitations of the format continued to multiply. The immediacy of the sessions gave the false impression that genuine insights were being exposed, but clarity was still elusive. That's when we turned to individual in-depth interviews as an alternative.

Different circumstances require different methodologies. In-depth interviews are particularly well suited to understanding complex situations, unlocking crucial emotional triggers, and providing the foundation for strategic planning. If executed well, they help organizations unearth issues they never thought to raise, resulting in a deeper and more nuanced understanding of those issues. Free of the constraints that plague focus groups, they provide a much richer opportunity for personal interaction. Because of the benefits they offer, it's tempting to think that all in-depth interviews are the same. They're not. The definition has been stretched to encompass anything from a 10-minute phone conversation to a face-to-face interview lasting more than an hour. Sometimes a prepared discussion guide based on a specific set of pre-determined topics is used in place of a survey questionnaire. In other instances, the meeting is less structured. The value of in-depth interviews depends on logistics, length, and format.

Logistics

We were repeatedly told that a big advantage of in-depth interviews was that they could be conducted by phone. Yes, but what a terrible idea! A voice on the other end of the phone isn't the same as sitting together in the same room. Without an opportunity for the interviewer to establish a personal connection and foster a sense of trust, people are more circumspect. It's also more difficult to engage someone when they're distracted by what's going on at the other end of the line. Conversations tend to be shorter, and they end more abruptly. Without the ability to observe body language, an interpretive component is missing.

"Ethnographic research" is a term used to describe interviews conducted in a person's home or office. This approach is based on the belief that spending time with individuals in their own environment leads to deeper insight because it's possible to observe behavior, physical settings, or body language the interviewer would not have seen during a phone conversation. This methodology is most appropriate for consumer-product companies that want to learn how tasks are performed or products are used. Insights they gain form the basis of future product research and development initiatives. The growing popularity of ethnographic research among consumer product companies reinforces the increased support for conducting interviews in-person.

Length

The length of an exchange also determines whether it qualifies as an in-depth interview. Conversations that last 10 to 20 minutes have, at times, been incorrectly positioned as in-depth interviews. They may be interviews, but they are certainly not in-depth. A short exchange may be useful to verify information from expert sources or obtain detailed factual answers, but short interviews don't provide enough time to address more complex issues.

Format

Typically, the format of traditional in-depth interviews is based on a prepared discussion guide consisting of specific, usually direct questions. Regardless of whether the questions are open-ended, we learned that the merit of in-depth interviews is diminished by strict adherence to a discussion guide, because it eclipses a more spontaneous exchange. Interviews driven by a fixed notion of what the topics should be, and how best to broach them, produce answers, not insights. In-depth interviews fall into this trap when interviewers, because of inexperience or inclination, resist deviating from what's been prepared in advance. Such shortcuts leave important issues unexamined, nuances lost, and key emotional triggers undetected. Instead, the exchange is prejudiced by what the interviewer, rather than the person being interviewed, thinks is relevant.

False Assumptions, Superficial Solutions

For many years, a major telecommunications company had been a leader in breakthrough technology. They were widely recognized and held in high esteem for their superior engineering applications. But through time, they had stopped innovating breakthrough products that were once at the core of their reputation for creative excellence. The company's senior executives were stumped. Why had this talented workforce lost their creative edge?

To answer that question, an outside company was hired to conduct a series of personal, in-depth interviews with a cross-section of key employees. But rather than starting with a blank slate, the interviewers took a narrow approach. They asked specific questions that someone decided, in advance, best defined the parameters of creativity. In particular, they focused on physical environment, sensory stimulation, and atmospherics.

Apparently, based on responses to these very specific questions, engineers lacked a retreat where they could gather and think. The company was told the answer was to open ideation centers outfitted with body hugging chairs, mind games, toys, books, music, and posters. A comfortable, pressure-free atmosphere that provided an abundance of sensory and intellectual stimulation would supposedly reignite the engineers' creative juices. So, the telecommunications company proceeded to open a number of such centers. But few engineers took advantage of them, and even more disheartening, nothing changed. There was still a dearth of exciting new ideas.

When the ideation centers failed, we were brought in to help management figure out how to reintroduce innovation to the workplace and restore the company's original cutting edge reputation. Obviously, a better understanding was needed of why employees' heads were down and their morale was low. So we conducted a second set of in-depth interviews throughout the organization.

These interviews revealed that years of strict cost-cutting and rigidly enforced controls had fostered a corporate culture defined by bureaucracy, complacency, and even fear. New ideas were not rewarded; the focus was on meeting deadlines and staying within budget. No amount of toys to play with would reinvigorate a workforce that was being praised for coloring between the lines and punished for their failure to do so. Employees felt they were living on borrowed time. Because they didn't believe they'd be around long term, they had little interest in thinking about products for the future.

Through the stories they shared, we learned how a once exciting environment infused with enthusiasm had changed. Their jobs had become mundane, and they lacked inspiration. The key to unlocking creativity wasn't about a physical place or filling a room with diversions. It was about something much bigger than that, something much more important. It was about their spirit.

The insights that were uncovered during these subsequent interviews alerted management to the severity of their problem and sparked a major effort to re-ignite innovation. Recommendations of how to reinforce creativity began with a plan to build upon an existing sub-culture of dynamic thinkers. Then a curriculum was developed for the ideation centers, transforming them from useless playrooms to destination locations for seminars, group discussions, and networking. Finally, and most importantly, we identified the policies and practices that discouraged innovation. Then we worked with management to change them.

It was clear from the original in-depth interviews that the spirit of creativity within this company had been lost, but the interviewers incorrectly perceived the cause to be about external factors, such as the physical work environment, gadgets, and games. A rigid dependence on a prepared discussion guide was the problem. Instead of first trying to understand the issue in a broader context, they had already decided what factors contributed to creativity, and then proceeded to essentially rate the company's performance on those factors. They were recording answers, they weren't mining for insights. They failed to delve deeply enough into the root causes of the problem. Superficial questions led to superficial responses, and those responses resulted in superficial solutions that turned out to be wrong.

Pros and Cons of In-Depth Interviews

The telecommunications experience demonstrated that in-depth interviews work best when the person being interviewed is allowed to take the lead.

IN-DEPTH INTERVIEWS ARE APPEALING BECAUSE:

- ☐ They are the most conducive format for probing and dissecting complex issues that are not clearly understood.
- ☐ They encourage lengthy narratives that reveal nuanced considerations in ways not previously explored.
- ☐ The findings, free of peer pressure evident in focus groups, are more honest.
- ☐ One-on-one conversations are best when discussing sensitive or confidential information.
- ☐ They expose emotional triggers in a context that leads to genuine insight.

TRADITIONAL IN-DEPTH INTERVIEWS FAIL BECAUSE:

- ☐ They are structured to validate a hypothesis by posing specific questions to test only that hypothesis.
- ☐ They represent someone else's assumptions of the most important issues or most relevant topic, not those of the person being interviewed.
- ☐ Questions on pre-determined topics provide answers rather than insights; they discourage spontaneous exchanges that lead to authentic emotional triggers.

A New Form of Research

It was only after analyzing all the available alternatives that we finally realized the answer had been in front of us all along. The best results we ever achieved happened when we employed in-depth interviews that relied on a string of open-ended provocative questions. The limited number of thought-provoking questions encouraged customers to speak in narratives. Unlike quantitative surveys or in-depth interviews that revolve around prepared discussion guides, narratives proved more valuable, because there were no built-in theories about the issues that might surface.

Surveys and discussion guides are based on speculation. They imagine possible answers and pose specific questions, accordingly. This in-depth interview technique, which was, in contrast, free of any pre-existing assumptions, helped break down complex issues in ways that were more easily understood. In the process, important and often unanticipated insights were exposed, forming the basis of successful strategic solutions.

This methodology became the cornerstone of our consulting practices. It is how we assist clients in their search for clarity and authentic insights, because it's an extremely effective way to expose emotional triggers. These emotional triggers consistently prove invaluable to solving business challenges. This powerful technique, emotional trigger research, is the better way.

Emotional-trigger research is not easy to successfully implement. It's not a trendy, value-added opportunity. It requires trained professionals with hard-edged business experience, who understand how to craft effective and pragmatic solutions based upon the insights this technique uncovers. It requires expertise in insightful listening, probing, and interpreting. Because this powerful methodology is also an unconventional one, it requires someone who has unlearned behaviors, beliefs, and lessons that businesses have relied upon as established practice when seeking to learn the truth.

As we go through the next 12 chapters, we'll share case studies with you that illustrate the power of emotional-trigger research. You'll see how this technique consistently helped a diverse group of organizations dissect complex issues, learn important new lessons, and use genuine insights, rather than answers to successfully achieve their objectives. All of the case studies that follow are true, but since client confidentiality is important to us and remains the cornerstone of our practices, minor details may have been changed to protect a company's identity.

Part II

Putting Emotional Triggers to Work—Sales

Chapter 4

Jumpstarting Sales

The Emotional Triggers That Solved the Mystery of a Weak Category

Using the bell curve to chart performance, most businesses inhabit the vast middle. Residing in a place equivalent to "average" has become risky. Years ago "average" suggested "solid." Not anymore; now

> It is easier to manufacture seven facts out of whole cloth than one emotion.
> —Mark Twain

the word is a red flag, warning of oncoming danger. The literal definition of "average" is "normal" or "typical." But that's not the connotation and it's rarely the reality. Today "average" is spelled "m-e-d-i-o-c-r-e," and mediocre organizations tend to simply peter out over time. This is the story about a company in such a predicament, because, although sales overall were decent, they continually missed projections in their most profitable product category. Their inability to jumpstart sales in this category put a damper on the bottom line. Emotional-trigger research solved the mystery of this underperforming category and provided the insights needed to turn the business around.

LESSON #1

> The context in which information is received drives opinions and actions.

An Inconvenient Truth

A leading national organization within the automotive aftermarket industry provided a combination of parts, supplies, and services to both the commercial and consumer sectors. In general, sales were good, but, no matter how aggressively this company marketed their quality assortment of private-label tires, they couldn't generate much enthusiasm.

Executives within the company couldn't understand the resistance to their private-label tires. It was a complete mystery. All the "facts" in their possession suggested sales should be better. It was quite inconvenient that reality had a nasty way of conflicting with these irrefutable "facts." In desperation, the decision was made to use emotional-trigger research to find out why customers were so unwilling to buy these tires.

An Unlikely Combination: Tires and Emotion

Many of you probably think the purchasing decision regarding tires is pretty cut and dry, making it a perfect candidate for a quantitative survey. After all, what could be more devoid of emotion that buying tires? We started out thinking that ourselves. Well we were wrong, and if you were thinking along the same lines as us, you'd be wrong too.

The Way It Was

This automotive aftermarket's extensive line of private-label tires was manufactured by a respected company within the industry. Tests conducted at the manufacturer's facility confirmed the performance of these tires ranked as good or in some cases better than comparable recognized brands. Additionally, they were priced 20 to 30 percent below those same national brands.

"They were absolutely convinced...the price differential would set them apart."

Executives believed the combination of favorable test results and significant savings made their tires the obvious choice. They were absolutely convinced, given the tires' performance parity with nationally recognized brands, the price differential would set them apart. For years, it was the principal thrust of all their marketing efforts.

They couldn't fathom why more tires weren't selling. Everyone was convinced the problem was with the advertising, marketing, or sales department. Someone wasn't plugging the benefits aggressively enough. The graphics weren't exciting enough. The comparable savings weren't obvious enough. The sales team wasn't convincing enough. Maybe their training program wasn't good enough. Or, a personal favorite, maybe the customers were just confused.

Price, Price, Price

To some degree, management was right about pricing. There were indeed price conscious customers always on the lookout for a "deal." Capturing these customers was easy. But there weren't enough of them, and, to make matters worse, they were the least-profitable customer segment. An exclusive emphasis on price failed to achieve the company's primary goal of increasing tire sales overall. Still, they remained committed to restricting their assortment to private-label tires, because they were more profitable than national brands, but, clearly, something had to change.

Management viewed price as an absolute. It wasn't. In fact, very few customers said they purchased tires somewhere else because they got a better price. The company had put all their eggs in the wrong basket. Emotional-trigger research revealed a strong disconnect between the company's assumptions and what customers valued. In fact, price was only a "deal clincher" when customers were convinced all the alternatives under consideration were identical. Otherwise, they chose the product that matched their exact requirements. Price was not a stand-alone issue.

Peace of Mind: Priceless!

The majority of customers, though not necessarily brand specific, were definitely brand focused. On an intellectual level, the customers participating in these interviews linked a name-brand tire with quality. But the emotional trigger was about something much more real, something infinitely more heartfelt. It was about that intangible longing for peace of mind. They assumed that major manufacturers of nationally recognized brands were reputable, had an established track record, and produced safe products. For them the "familiar" carried the implication of "reliable;" the unfamiliar made them nervous.

These customers understood the concept of private-label merchandise. Most of them routinely bought store branded apparel, groceries, or household products without giving it a second thought. But they were far less casual when it came to the company's line of private-label tires. A poor decision could directly jeopardize their safety or their family's safety. That was why they refused to buy them. As far as they were concerned, the tires were unproven. They really didn't know much about them.

No other emotional trigger impacted the automotive aftermarket company's ability to increase tire sales more than peace of mind. It outweighed all other considerations. Purchasing a private-label can of peaches or T-shirt from a local department store was one thing. Putting themselves or their family, particularly their children, in a situation that might be dangerous was quite another. Car accidents often resulted in serious injuries, even death. The stakes were too high, and nothing they had seen or heard was sufficient to reassure them. Then there was another factor. Counter-balancing the desire for peace of mind was an equally strong, negative emotional trigger: skepticism.

Gaining a comfort level with these private-label tires demanded more than a good sales pitch, eye-catching product literature, or advertising. Customers wanted information in "context." They didn't trust the results of tests conducted by the manufacturer. They needed third party assurances that specifically compared these tires to major national brands and certified that the performance and safety were every bit as good. Only hard "evidence" from legitimate independent testing facilities would convince them.

Previous research had repeatedly documented customer resistance to purchasing the private-label tires. Quantitative studies were framed exclusively as statistics, rankings, and ratings, while focus groups were no more helpful. Reasons were provided, but "actionable" insight was missing.

Emotional-trigger research dispelled the notion that tires were a purely objective purchase decision based on the sharpest prices, the manufacturer's test results, or the best advertising. In reality, it was a highly charged issue that centered on peace of mind. Unless that need was satisfied, there would be no realistic chance to boost sales.

Tellingly, each of the key emotional triggers came across as a strong need.

EMOTIONAL TRIGGER	WHAT EMOTIONAL TRIGGERS REVEALED
Needs	▢ Above all, customers needed peace of mind. They simply wouldn't entrust their safety, or more importantly, the safety of their family, to a product they considered unproven. The risks associated with driving on inferior tires were too great. ▢ Customers needed reassurance, which could be gained through proof. They needed to know their decision was based on information that came from a source with no vested interest in their purchase decision. They believed an independent source had their best interest at heart. ▢ Customers needed to able to trust that what they were being told was the truth. If they were unsure, the unknown was too frightening.

The Answer

When the need for peace of mind was revealed, it became possible to go beyond what was merely accurate and focus instead on what was real. It enabled the automotive aftermarket company to dispense with "solutions" based on internally held assumptions or on a misinterpretation of the "facts." Now they were positioned to focus on what really mattered most to their customers.

"The key was to hire a respected independent testing facility that customers would know and trust."

A winning strategy required proof that the quality and performance of the private-label tires were equal to nationally recognized brands. The key was to hire a respected independent testing facility that customers would know and trust. When this facility confirmed the private-label tires were as good as leading national brands, it would provide the element of credibility that was missing. This was the "impartial" endorsement the company needed to increase sales and to initiate an aggressive marketing campaign focused on the right issue. At every point of customer contact, the testing results were the "ammunition" for reassuring customers and giving them peace of mind.

Once the truth was known, the solutions presented themselves: Use advertising to publicize the name of the testing facility and the results. Include performance and quality comparisons with each of the leading national brands. Emphasize the testing facility's credentials and as well as promoting favorable results in collateral sales material. Train the sales team on how to position the features and benefits of the private-label tires. Teach them how to frame the testing results in response to the most important emotional triggers. Finally, post the testing facility's findings prominently on the company's Website.

Emotional-trigger research provided a path to a more profitable future. It demonstrated that customer values are not abstract or objective, but very subjective. Although standard industry logic suggested price and performance were the key customer considerations, their emotional triggers were actually trust and outside validation. Opinions were formed and actions were based on the "context" in which information was received.

SUMMING UP:
JUMPSTARTING SALES

Situation

A leading national automotive aftermarket company providing parts, supplies, and services experienced only modest success. An inability to jumpstart sales in their most profitable category put a damper on the bottom line. For years, their private-label tires, manufactured by a respected industry leader, missed sales projections. According to the manufacturer's tests, quality and performance were comparable to the major, recognized brands, but the tires sold for 20 to 30 percent less. Given the price differential, the company believed it to be their competitive advantage and made it the focus of their marketing efforts. Although promoting price enabled the company to capture the least profitable "bargain hunters," it did nothing to increase sales overall. Emotional-trigger research was conducted with existing customers that had never purchased the private-label tires to find out why they hadn't.

The Customers' Emotional Triggers

Most customers weren't knowledgeable about tires and, given the safety issues, needed reassurance. The potential risk associated with making the wrong decision frightened them. They needed to trust the information they were given and the source of that information.

Genuine Insight

Customers believed the manufacturer's test results were clouded by self-interest. When they bought tires, the safety of their families was a top priority. Because of the potentially serious consequences of driving on poor quality tires, price alone was not the determining factor. The marketing strategy had to address peace of mind.

Solution

Peace of mind was the emotional trigger than unlocked the mystery of this underperforming category. The solution was to retain a highly regarded and well-known independent testing facility to document that these private-label tires were comparable, in both quality and performance, to the nationally recognized brands. This was the missing impartial and credible endorsement the company needed. Once armed with legitimate proof, the findings provided the ammunition to launch an aggressive three-pronged advertising, marketing, and sales initiative.

Chapter 5

Acquiring New Customers

The Emotional Triggers That Transformed a Sales Organization

Sometimes a company is their own worst enemy. The competition isn't the problem. Instead, it creates obstacles all on its own. This is the story of a Southwest data storage operation that found their service extremely timely following Hurricane Katrina. Their top-notch sales team easily opened doors with companies more acutely aware of the need to protect sensitive data, but they failed to gain many new customers. Emotional-trigger research revealed the fatal flaw in their sales approach and provided the insights that transformed their business.

> The human body has two ears and one mouth. To be good at persuading or selling, you must learn to use those natural devices in proportion.
>
> —Tom Hopkins

LESSON #2

> Focus on what the customer wants, not what you want them to want.

85

Stars in Alignment

Companies looking to store their electronic data have three choices. They can store it in a safe place within their own building, they can elect to store it off site as an added safety measure, or they can do both. Whatever decision they make, the need to protect vital information represents a growing opportunity for data storage companies. A smart entrepreneur, recognizing the increasing need for such a service, decided to enter this highly competitive business.

Filled with enthusiasm, the president implemented the necessary steps to ensure his company's success. He began by hiring an eager, young sales team and training these bright recruits on the art of consultative selling. His new facility was state-of-the-art. All the pieces seemed to be in place.

Then, without warning, a catastrophic event catapulted his service into a top priority throughout the region. Following Hurricane Katrina, companies devastated by the loss of their data or unnerved by stories of other companies' losses, were frantically seeking ways to protect critical information. An unspeakable tragedy had suddenly created an even greater demand for off-site data storage. Chief information officers were under tremendous pressure from top management to ensure the safety of their company's crucial data...and fast! What ensued within the marketplace was beyond the president's wildest dreams.

An Unexpected Surprise

Given the circumstances, the owner of the data storage company naturally expected his business to experience a dramatic growth spurt. But the "spurt" was definitely "sputtering." What was going on? He was completely baffled and more than a little distressed. Potential customers were lining up to talk with his sales team. Doors literally flung open from one end of town to the other. The competition was growing by leaps and bounds. But this start-up's closure rate for new business was extremely low.

As we've said, the equipment was state-of-the-art. The location was convenient and the organization was infused with a positive "can do" attitude. The sales team, by all accounts, was impressive. The sales materials were relevant, as well as compelling. Most important of all, they had a service everyone wanted. Things were supposed to be going better, much better.

Chief information officers understood the real calamity that awaited them if their company's data was destroyed or contaminated; they were very motivated individuals. The data storage company should have been turning away business. Instead, they were being turned away. Management and the sales team tried to second guess themselves. Maybe they were too expensive. Maybe they weren't strategic enough with clients focused on both technical and physical needs. Maybe their knowledge was too limited. Maybe they didn't adequately present an overall picture of the pros and cons customers wanted, or maybe the conversations weren't "dynamic" enough. The explanations they came up with were pure conjecture, hardly a reasonable basis for implementing change.

> **"Management and the sales team tried to second guess themselves. The explanations they came up with were pure conjecture, hardly a reasonable basis for implementing change."**

This start-up needed help, and management was the first to admit it. The president decided to commission an emotional-trigger research study to understand why their closure rate was so low and how they could improve it.

A Multitude of Voices, a Single Complaint

Potential clients expressed a sense of relief when the sales team requested an appointment. Organizations everywhere were looking for a fail-safe plan. As we've explained, technology executives were on the hot seat. But regardless of how much they were a "client in search of a solution," they all related similar stories of how the start-up data storage company was their own worst enemy.

When this company called on a prospective customer, a member of the sales team and the technical sales expert both attended the meeting. The sales rep "pitched" the business reasons for using their service. The technical expert was there to answer specific technology questions. Prospects agreed the salespeople were friendly, tenacious, accommodating, and smart. They liked their demeanor, felt personally comfortable with them, and overall had only positive comments about their approach to the business. Likewise, they expressed confidence that the technical expert had a solid grasp of their issues and how to tackle them. So far, so good.

Initially, everyone had felt optimistic during their first encounter. Potential customers held high hopes for a future association. Then things started to fall apart. Why? Well, the short answer was that it took too long to close the sale. But what exactly did that mean? And, more to the point, why did it take so long? How was the data storage company snatching defeat from the jaws of victory?

Probing deeper, prospects were encouraged to describe their experiences at length. They spoke in one voice as they began to relate, step by step, what they characterized as an "excruciatingly laborious" process to reach agreement. The sales rep kicked off the meeting by presenting an overview of the data storage company including their capabilities and their state-of-the-art facility. Customers were assured data would be secure and were asked if they had any questions. Theoretically, the technical expert was on hand to answer any specific technology related questions that arose. At least that was the plan, but it wasn't what happened.

Instead of focusing on the prospect's interests and priorities, the technical expert had his own agenda. Invariably, things got bogged down when he began talking. He went on and on, completely taking over the meeting. First, he elaborated on the company's technical capabilities. Then, he launched into a lengthy discussion of broad technology issues in general. Customers' eyes started to glaze over, but he was oblivious. He was so busy talking, he never even took notes.

Making matters worse, the more the conversation veered toward technology solutions, the more the sales reps withdrew from the exchange. Essentially, they abdicated their role as the "lead" liaison with the customer and permitted the technical expert to control the agenda. Worse still, by default, they empowered their technical partner to define the scope of the project, determine the next steps, and make commitments regarding the time frames and deliverables for the subsequent proposal. He collected the pertinent information and assumed responsibility for writing the proposal. Then he submitted it to the potential customer, without ever showing it to the "lead" sales rep.

Time after time, prospect after prospect, their stories were always the same. When the proposal was submitted, it bore little resemblance to what the customer had originally requested. Without exception, the project scope always mushroomed into something much larger and more complex than what was expected. Prospects may only have needed a Chevy, but they were getting a Cadillac, whether they wanted one or not. Every proposal came adorned with a complete set of "bells and whistles." No expense was spared. Nothing was too good for his potential customers.

Can You Hear Me Now?

How infuriating! Prospects were frustrated. They had spent considerable time defining their needs. When the sales team left their office after that first meeting, they believed everyone had a clear understanding of what the proposal should contain. Who changed the parameters, and why weren't they consulted? Then the dance began. Customers contacted the technical expert requesting revisions. Again, they received a proposal that exceeded their requirements. So, they called a second time. And a third. Maybe even a fourth.

Frustration quickly escalated to exasperation, and then to anger. They were wasting time, precious time. Progress was bogged down by one communications breakdown after another.

The technical expert apparently had his own ideas and his own bias. He repeatedly submitted proposals based on what he thought customers should want instead of what they actually wanted. Sometimes weeks passed, as four or more rewrites traveled back and forth. Finally, prospects at a loss to understand the reason for the disconnect, and by now completely disgusted, terminated the conversation and gave their business to a competitor.

The emotional triggers were unmistakable. Prospects spoke with one voice, related similar experiences, and shared common feelings.

Emotional Trigger	What Emotional Triggers Revealed
Patterns of Behavior	□ They met with the sales rep and the technical expert. They agreed on the specifications for a proposal, but what the technical expert submitted bore no resemblance to what had been requested. So he submitted a revision, but it was still different from what the customer had discussed. Then he proceeded to submit another revision. And one more after that. Each proposal was based on what the technical expert thought should be included.

Needs	□ They needed a rapid solution to assure their management that they were on top of a sensitive issue.
	□ They needed tangible evidence that their priorities came first.
Feeling	□ They felt pressured by their bosses to secure their company's vital data.
	□ They felt irritated that the initial proposal did not reflect their needs.
Experiences	□ They experienced deep frustration, because the technical expert wasted their time and deliberately failed to incorporate the changes they requested after repeated conversations.
	□ They experienced a process that was both "excruciatingly laborious" and "redundant."

What Went Wrong?

Emotional-trigger research interviews provided the genuine insight at the heart of the data-storage company's problem. They had lost sight of their ultimate objective and, as a result, failed to lead with their strength. The sales team was the group responsible for opening doors and signing new accounts. The technical partner was included in the meeting to address specific technology issues as appropriate. By allowing their roles to be reversed, the sales team had quite literally relinquished all control.

When the technical expert failed to ask enough probing questions during the initial meeting, they didn't intercede. When he went off on tangents, they didn't stop him. When he wrote the proposal, they didn't review it. When he submitted up to four revisions, they didn't step in to figure out what was going wrong. The sales team was intimidated by their technical partner's expertise. After the first meeting they just assumed he'd submit the proposal and close the sale. And when he failed to "seal the deal" time and again, they simply accepted the disappointment, moving on to the next prospect without ever looking back.

Setting Things Right

Bottom line, there was no oversight. There was no internal review process to ensure the sales team examined every proposal in advance and made sure it complied with the customer's instructions. Had such a system been in place, the sales team would have known the proposals were inconsistent with the assignment. But without a formalized process, the sales team often had no idea how many times a proposal was actually revised.

Once the president understood the source of the problem, he immediately went about solving it. First he met with the sales team and the technical expert. In no uncertain terms, he reiterated the sales team was in charge of new business development. They were responsible for running meetings, writing proposals, and ensuring each proposal was consistent with the prospect's requirements. It was their sole responsibility to close the deal. The technical expert was just that: a technical expert. He was there to provide technical expertise, when needed. It was not his job to define project parameters. Nor was it up to him to decide want customers should want.

Checks and balances were put in place to guarantee no proposal was sent out until the technical expert verified the accuracy of any technical details contained within the document. However, it was the sales rep who made sure every aspect of the proposal specifically addressed what the customer had outlined. The sales rep also took charge of writing the proposal, submitting it on time, and following up with potential customers to ensure it was on target.

Within just a few days of implementing these changes, the data storage company signed a multi-million-dollar account. Within one year, they had exceeded their sales goal by 30 percent.

Emotional-trigger research uncovered deep-rooted organizational problems that the sales team and the technical sales expert failed to recognize or chose to ignore. But once those hidden reasons were exposed, unfiltered through the prism of inside out thinking, the president was able to implement the changes that transformed his sales organization.

SUMMING UP
ACQUIRING NEW CUSTOMERS

Situation

A smart and aggressive entrepreneur entered the competitive data storage business in a major Southwest city. He opened a state-of-the-art facility and trained his team on consultative selling. Then Hurricane Katrina hit, and suddenly the demand for off-site storage exploded. But while the competition was growing by leaps and bounds, his company's closure rate for new business remained low. Typically, the data storage company sent a technical expert, along with the sales representative, to new business pitches. The sales rep was responsible for presenting the company's services, and the technical partner's role was to answer specific technology questions. Chief information officers, under tremendous pressure to secure their company's vital data, were motivated customers. Although doors literally flung open when the data storage company requested an initial meeting, they acquired few new accounts. The president commissioned emotional-trigger research to learn why their closure rate was so low and how they could to fix it.

The Customers' Emotional Triggers

Customers, initially impressed with the sales team and confident the technical expert had a grasp of their needs, quickly became frustrated when the technical expert stepped in and dominated the meeting. Then he submitted proposal after proposal that exceeded their specifications. Frustration turned to anger, as time was wasted and no progress was made. Feeling enormous pressure to assure management their company's data was safe, customers finally went with a competitive service.

Genuine Insight

The sales team, intimidated by their technical partner's expertise, had abdicated control of the entire process. They weren't proactive and failed to keep their technical partner in check. By tacitly agreeing to a reversal of their roles, customer needs went unmet and the new business closure rate suffered.

Solution

Once it became apparent that the sales process revolved around the technical expert's bias, instead of the customer's needs, the course correction was clear. The president demanded the sales team accept responsibility for running the meeting, writing the proposal, and following up with customers to close the deal. The technical expert's participation was limited to answering technology questions and verifying the accuracy of specific details in the proposal. Within days of implementing the changes, the company signed a new multi-million-dollar account. A year later, they had exceeded their sales goal by 30 percent.

Chapter 6

Winning More Business From Existing Customers

The Emotional Triggers That Captured Senior Management Attention

Every so often, a company gets really lucky, because the demand for their product or service is driven by external forces. This is the story about such a business. They were literally sitting on a gold mine and didn't realize it. Emotional-trigger research exposed key insights that enabled this company to capitalize on untapped opportunities and elevate their level

> Sometimes the situation is only a problem because it is looked at in a certain way. Looked at in another way, the right course of action may be so obvious that the problem no longer exists.
>
> —Edward de Bono

of client contact to senior decision makers. By repositioning their service as the answer to new government regulations, chief financial officers embraced them as the answer to their problem and awarded them more business.

LESSON #3

One company's problem is another company's opportunity.

95

A New Business Model

As this story begins, online auction sites for surplus oil and gas industry equipment were in their infancy. Within five years, one particular site had grown from a start-up operation to a $25 million business, serving the needs of corporations ranging from the four major oil companies to smaller national and regional concerns. They appeared to have unlimited potential. Sales were going in the right direction: up.

Full of entrepreneurial zeal and optimistic about the future, the company president wanted to build his business even faster. But he needed help. He needed to clarify how best to satisfy current customers. He needed a better understanding of how decisions were made within the large corporations he served. And, he especially needed insights regarding how his company was perceived within the industry and how best to position his offering as the value-added alternative. He turned to emotional-trigger research for direction.

Follow the Money

Because this company was specifically focused on discovering unidentified opportunities to grow its business, the decision was made to interview senior executives who controlled the purse strings. Chief financial officers were the logical choice. They were responsible for excess inventory, and the online auction site served as a centralized resource for liquidating surplus equipment. Chief financial officers from a cross-section of companies were interviewed. The objective was to understand how their world was changing, how those changes affected their priorities, and the implication of those new priorities for the president of the online auction site.

So Much Activity, So Little Control

Considering how much money large corporations spent on major equipment, their approach to managing excess inventory was often surprisingly casual. Typically oil and gas companies were structured by project. Each project leader had his own budget and managed his own profit and loss statement. He purchased his own equipment, and, when it was no longer needed, decided what to do with it. Project teams were free to choose one of four solutions: warehouse the equipment, sell it at a live auction, use the online auction site, or sell it at one of several company lots. Frequently, large corporations lacked uniform guidelines or had no centralized system in place to track the surplus equipment they disposed of. As a result, many companies had inadequate inventory control.

Prior to the emotional-trigger research assignment, the online auction site was barely on the CFO's radar screen. Some had a vague awareness of the service, but none had any direct involvement. Lower-level personnel on project teams or company lot managers might have sold limited amounts of equipment on the online site, but it was a hit-or-miss proposition. There were few company-wide coordination efforts.

A Gathering Storm: Sarbanes-Oxley

Then everything changed. Federal legislation was passed that rocked the world of these chief financial officers; the Sarbanes-Oxley Act, also known as the Public Company Accounting Reform and Investor Protection Act of 2002, became law. This law introduced new or enhanced standards for all boards, management, and accounting firms of publicly traded U.S. companies. In particular, there was a provision that required public companies to evaluate and disclose the effectiveness of their internal controls as they related to financial reporting. Both chief executive officers and chief financial officers were required to certify the accuracy of all financial reports issued by their companies. Misrepresentation,

"...failure to comply carried the threat of corporate fines and possibly criminal penalties. With the stroke of a pen, lax inventory controls suddenly became a potential nightmare."

incomplete documentation, or failure to comply carried the threat of corporate fines and possibly criminal penalties.

With the stroke of a pen, lax inventory controls suddenly became a potential nightmare. If chief financial officers were unable to account for all the surplus equipment that was either sold or warehoused throughout their organization, they couldn't accurately report the total value of corporate assets, and failure to do so would place them in violation of federally mandated financial disclosure laws. What had once been an administrative challenge was now a much more serious matter. Sarbanes-Oxley had their total attention.

Drowning in a Sea of Regulations

Chief financial officers were overwhelmed by the magnitude of the new Sarbanes-Oxley requirements. They knew their jobs were in jeopardy if they couldn't get a handle on the inventory control issue. But where should they start? At many companies, disposal of surplus equipment had been handled on a decentralized basis for many years. Now this sweeping new legislation demanded a complete and rapid overhaul of how inventory was managed and tracked.

But large corporations move slowly and that only added to the chief financial officers' anxiety. The pressures they were under personally were at

"The pressures they were under personally were at odds with their companies' ability to manage change quickly."

odds with their companies' ability to manage such rapid change. As they started to discuss the variety of methods used to deal with surplus equipment, they began to realize the full scope of the problem they were confronting.

Most companies maintained multiple lots, where they sold a certain amount of equipment. But few had put a comprehensive tracking system in place to account for everything that was sold. These lots were managed by "gatekeepers" who, on occasion, had a different agenda than their employer. A dishonest lot manager might line his pockets by selling equipment on the side. Under the current arrangement there was little oversight. And, without a centralized system to control the process, it was very difficult for a chief financial officer to identify funds skimmed off the top.

Live auctions presented other problems. Logistics were a hassle. Equipment had to be transported to the actual location so potential buyers could inspect it. Complicating matters, equipment might be sold before the auction officially began and companies often didn't know who bought it or what they paid. Every transaction wasn't transparent. The project group that auctioned off the equipment received a recap, but that report was rarely submitted to the chief financial officer.

Chief financial officers were feeling the pressure of Sarbanes-Oxley from every angle. Compliance deadlines were looming. It was all new and unfamiliar. Potential consequences were staggering. It was unlikely their companies would be able to implement change as quickly as the new law dictated.

Connecting the Dots

The president of the online auction site had built his business by establishing relationships with individual project managers and lot "gatekeepers" at various oil and gas companies. His sales team called on these customers regularly, hoping to convince them to use the online site whenever they had surplus equipment to unload. They were trained to sell a service, nothing more.

Lower-level project managers and lot "gatekeepers" were probably unfamiliar with the ramifications of Sarbanes-Oxley. Perhaps they were unaware of the legislation, or maybe they just didn't care. In any event, because it wasn't their priority, it had little bearing on the arrangements they made to sell surplus equipment. The online site's sales team was equally out of the loop. Regardless of whether or not they knew about Sarbanes-Oxley, they hadn't connected the dots and realized the enormous impact it could have on their business.

By focusing on tactical sales transactions with personnel in lower levels within the organization, they had failed to recognize an exciting new opportunity. Emotional-trigger research clarified how the online auction site could win more business from current customers by setting up their company as the potential solution to every chief financial officer's problem. If communicated correctly, chief financial officers would appreciate they had a vested interest in meeting directly with representatives of the online site, rather than delegating the responsibility to more junior employees.

Talk about luck! Chief financial officers had a pressing need to streamline and centralize the disposal of surplus equipment. They also had the authority to make company-wide decisions. The online site stood to be a major beneficiary. But first, they had to reposition their business.

Emotional-trigger research uncovered the extent to which the chief financial officers lived and breathed Sarbanes-Oxley when the legislation first went into law. It consumed their days and kept them awake at night. Finding themselves on unfamiliar turf unleashed strong emotional triggers.

Emotional Trigger	What Emotional Triggers Revealed
Feelings	☐ They felt vulnerable. If they were unable to get a timely handle on their company's surplus equipment, they could lose their job. ☐ They felt overwhelmed by the scope of their responsibility. It was their legal obligation to account for and accurately value the company's surplus inventory, but they didn't know how to go about tackling it. ☐ They felt extremely anxious. They knew their personal time constraints were at odds with their company's inability to manage such rapid change. ☐ They felt frightened. Failure to comply with Sarbanes-Oxley carried the threat of corporate fines and/or criminal penalties.
Needs	☐ They needed to have hope. ☐ They needed a helping hand, a practical way to streamline accountability for their entire surplus inventory.

Repositioning the Online Auction Site as a Turnkey Solution

Operationally, Sarbanes-Oxley created a huge time sensitive problem for chief financial officers. Personally, it fostered feelings of anxiety and vulnerability. The combination of corporate pressure and personal unease made them more open than usual to fresh ideas and new solutions.

Emotional-trigger research offered genuine insights that enabled the online auction site to carve out a unique niche for their business. The decentralized approach to selling excess inventory had serious drawbacks. At the front end, chief financial officers couldn't manage the cost. They had no control over what their equipment sold for. At the back end, they had incomplete records, which hampered their ability to analyze the financial results. Reports were rarely sent to the CFO. Beyond that, even if the accuracy of every transaction could be established, gathering the required information from so many different sources was too extensive of an undertaking.

The oil and gas companies' problem became the online auction site's expansion opportunity. It enabled them to position their business as a transparent turnkey solution. The ease of selling surplus inventory online and tracking the sale from start to finish would hold up under scrutiny, because everything was electronically recorded for all to see. Financial transactions were streamlined in one place. Funds were collected and dispersed centrally. Large corporations no longer had to depend on project managers, company lot "gatekeepers," or managers of live auctions for reports and payments. Because the auction took place in real time, chief financial officers could log onto the site and observe any sales transaction. They no longer had to depend on a third party. The entire process was simplified, and they were assured of receiving legally verifiable documentation.

Targeting the Chief Financial Officer

Once the strategy of repositioning the business was agreed upon, the next step was to elevate the level of customer contact within the oil and gas companies. Rather than calling on project managers or company lot "gatekeepers," the focus shifted to chief financial officers, who were empowered to make corporate decisions regarding what to do with all excess inventory.

The president of the online auction site immediately began preparing his organization to work directly with chief financial officers. He brought in a Sarbanes-Oxley authority to familiarize the entire sales team with the requirements and ramifications of the legislation. Then he retained an expert to train his staff on solution selling. Because his team had previously dealt with lower level employees, many needed to develop more sophisticated, conceptual presentation and sales skills.

Recognizing this strategy depended on elevating the level of customer contact and successfully engaging senior management, the president went beyond training existing staff. He replaced employees not up to the task, upgrading the caliber and expertise of those who would be calling on chief financial officers.

All the sales and marketing materials were overhauled. The new focus emphasized the oil and gas companies' need to comply with Sarbanes-Oxley. Once everything was in place, the sales team began contacting the chief financial officers of companies they were already doing business with. They requested appointments to discuss how the online site provided a turnkey solution to Sarbanes-Oxley.

Chief financial officers made the connection instantly between the way they were currently handling excess inventory and the turnkey transparency the online auction site offered. Their response was one of immediate relief. Sales skyrocketed. Within two years the company doubled their sales.

Summing Up
Winning More Business From Current Customers

Situation

An online auction site for surplus oil and gas industry equipment had gone from a start-up to a $25 million business within five years. Pleased with that achievement but eager to grow even faster, the president turned to emotional-trigger research to discover untapped opportunities. Up to this point oil and gas companies had a decentralized approach to disposing of surplus equipment. As a result, transaction records were often spotty and usually remained with the group that had initiated the sale. Then Sarbanes-Oxley became law and suddenly chief financial officers, who had the responsibility for inventory management, were required, under penalty of corporate fines and criminal charges, to accurately report on the value of all company assets. But many didn't know how to go about changing a decentralized corporate culture as quickly as the law demanded. In order to understand the bigger picture, emotional-trigger research interviews were conducted with senior executives who were charged with managing corporate assets to learn how Sarbanes-Oxley was changing their world and the implications of those changes for the online auction site.

The Customers' Emotional Triggers

These corporate executives felt completely overwhelmed. They didn't know how to account for all their companies' excess inventory, how to verify the accuracy of reports submitted from various sources throughout their organization, or how to streamline a cumbersome manual task and coordinate all the information.

Genuine Insight

Given the vulnerability of these executives, it opened a door for the online auction site to reposition their company from a service business to a transparent Sarbanes-Oxley turnkey solution. By doing so, they could elevate the level of their client contact from lower level employees to senior management and win more business from existing and new accounts.

Solution

The company upgraded and trained their sales team on Sarbanes-Oxley and consultative selling. Sales materials were overhauled to specifically reposition the online auction site as the turnkey solution to the demands of Sarbanes-Oxley. Meetings were held with the CFO of existing customers to explain how their service offered complete transparency, with comprehensive and accurate reports from start to finish. The repositioned offering doubled their sales within two years.

Chapter 7

Selling a Company to High Priority Recruits

The Emotional Triggers That Doubled Acceptance Rates Among Top Talent

Values and priorities change with every generation. In particular, today's batch of college graduates takes a holistic view of life and work decisions. This is the story about a leading global manufacturer of precision tools that suddenly encountered a significant drop in acceptance rates among top-tier engineering graduates. Emotional-trigger research uncovered the reason they were attracting so few of their high priority candidates by clarifying the difference between what this generation valued and what the manufacturer, steeped in tradition, continued to offer. Once the company incorporated student priorities into their recruitment packages, they doubled the acceptance rate.

> Confidence is what you feel when you comprehend the situation.
> —Proverb

LESSON #4

> Market your company as more than a job. Market it as a balanced life experience.

The Whole World in Your Hands

For generations, the nation's best and brightest engineering graduates vied for an employment offer from this renowned international manufacturer of precision tools. It was a highly coveted prize, the brass ring. Undeniably, being associated with such a company was prestigious, but the real draw was an employment package that offered adventure, excitement, and unlimited possibilities.

Ultimately, the "chosen few" who joined this elite group of engineers jumped at the chance to participate in the company's highly structured, but time-tested, career path. They readily agreed to the stipulation that they relocate to far-flung locations every few years. Taking on different assignments and gaining new experiences in the process was an exhilarating prospect. They welcomed the opportunity to expand their horizons, achieve a more sophisticated global perspective, and have as many adventures as possible. What could be better?

Throughout the company's long esteemed history, the arrangement served the interests of both employee and employer. Talented young recruits seeking to spread their wings were able to fulfill their personal ambitions. They'd be able to see how other people lived and visit places they had only read about. They could join the company and see the world. It was a dream come true for those who resisted the routine, preferring the unknown and the unusual.

At the same time, the manufacturer had found an ideal way to transfer knowledge between divisions and reduce tensions among an international staff that did not share the same beliefs, traditions, or life experiences. They had successfully created a world class workforce that was the envy of their industry. Geographically and ethnically diverse, this workforce demonstrated a high level of tolerance for individual differences and an enthusiasm for embracing new ways.

Although the very notion of change threatened so many other companies, this global manufacturer found it easier to manage.

That's because change was deliberately "built" into the engineers' jobs. In so doing, it ensured the experience young recruits gained in one part of the world transferred seamlessly, as they moved from assignment to assignment. This strategy proved an effective method of sharing knowledge and fostering tolerance.

Have We Got a Deal for You

Then something unexpected happened. Baby Boomers aged. The face of new recruits began to change. For the first time, as the manufacturer prepared once again to cherry-pick the best and brightest of the next generation, they were met with resistance. The promise of a fast-track career, based on travel and diverse life experiences, failed to attract the children of Baby Boomers. Rather than clamoring to climb aboard, many young engineering recruits chose to go elsewhere.

The manufacturer was incredulous. The employment package they offered was "extremely attractive," the compensation more than competitive. So why wasn't it working? Why were these talented recruits turning down such a good deal? No longer able to attract the same high caliber engineering graduates upon whom the company had built its reputation, and at a complete loss as to why, top management turned to emotional-trigger research to identify the issues and the solutions to help reverse this alarming trend.

It Was Good Enough for Your Parents

Past generations, specifically Baby Boomers, were eager to live and work in new places. For the most part, they had grown up during a period of relative calm. Typically, their mother was a stay at home mom and their father was home most nights for dinner. If the family traveled, it was usually by car and limited to destinations within the United States. Their lives had been safe, sheltered, and predictable. But as young adults, safe, sheltered, and predictable translated to boring. It was the last thing they wanted. Upon graduating from college, they were ready to bolt from their cocoon.

Breaking free of the tethers that characterized their childhood was the defining emotional trigger that drove the decisions of these Baby Boomers. Shrewdly, the global manufacturer exploited that trigger to attract and retain the best engineering graduates throughout the country. The company's recruitment package featured an enticing combination of personal and financial benefits.

Salaries and bonuses were extremely generous. Favorable exchange rates offered a big tax advantage to expatriates working abroad. The home visit policy was very liberal. Joining a global manufacturer guaranteed young recruits a variety of interesting work experiences. Further, they were assured that the more countries in which they agreed to live, the more valuable they would be as an employee. Their willingness to relocate every few years was inextricably linked to an upwardly mobile career trajectory.

The offer appealed to young engineering recruits who didn't hesitate to assume a nomadic existence in exchange for adventure and monetary reward. The bargain they struck marked the beginning of a decades-long commitment to making their career a top priority. It was a bargain they struck willingly for the prestige, power, and wealth that came with success.

> **"The bargain they struck marked the beginning of a decades-long commitment to making their career their top priority."**

They're Our Lives and We'll Do What We Want

Imagine the global manufacturer's shock when so many children of Baby Boomers, the very people who had so passionately accepted the company's employment package, turned away in droves. They weren't enticed by extensive travel. They had little desire to live in far-off lands and dismissed the "pay your dues" expectation that they should. Their primary focus wasn't on a fast-track career. Money wasn't their only consideration. Infuriatingly, they just couldn't be bought.

Top-tier engineering recruits were more sophisticated and savvy than their parents had been at the same age. They had definite ideas about what they wanted. They were under no illusions about the tradeoffs involved. Much to the company's distress, the parents of these graduates often represented the quintessential role model of everything their children disliked about business. No, this group intended to blaze their own trail, and it was a trail unlike any the global manufacturer had encountered before.

Home Sweet Home

Although many of their parents had seen little of the world during their formative years, that was not the case with the majority of younger recruits. Some had already lived abroad with their parents and knew firsthand what that was like. Others had traveled overseas with their families as children or with friends as young adults. Many more had moved frequently within the United States, when their parents were promoted or started a new job. Products of a global society that was vastly different than the one Baby Boomers had experienced, multiculturalism held less fascination, because it wasn't shrouded in mystery. It was a routine part of their daily existence.

As these young recruits shared stories about their childhood and recounted their hopes for the future, it became clear that the emotional triggers shaping their world view represented a stark contrast to those of their parents. In fact, the choices they made represented the polar opposite of what their parents had wanted, believed, or cared about most. The global manufacturer was unprepared for this sea change. As a company steeped in an ethic that hard work and sacrifice was the way to achieve the American dream, they were stunned to discover that advancement and prosperity were not necessarily the emotional triggers most important to these talented engineering graduates.

Moving overseas, living in many different countries, or relocating frequently within the United States represented a powerful emotional trigger for career-oriented Baby Boomers and their children alike, but there was an ironic difference. Although it was a positive trigger for the older generation, it was an extremely negative one for many of the generation that followed.

When potential recruits reminisced about their experiences living in different parts of the world or transferring around the United States, their stories evoked neither adventure nor excitement as the central emotional trigger. For them, such experiences conjured up memories of loneliness, insecurity, and, at times, fear. Among those who had lived abroad, many recalled feeling uncomfortable in a strange country, where the language and customs were unfamiliar. They hated being treated as outsiders by other students. What they really wanted and needed was a support system to help them cope.

Regardless of where they grew up, constantly transferring from school to school or community to community, this younger generation of high priority recruits had vivid recollections of feeling left out, different, and unwelcome. They had no desire to repeat a similar experience as adults, nor

"Those who had been up-rooted yearned to establish roots."

did they have any intention of inflicting the same emotional burden on their families. Security and stability were dominant emotional triggers. They longed for a home within a community where they and their children could become part of a caring, comfortable, and nurturing extended family. Those who had been uprooted yearned to establish roots.

Yet the emotional triggers that explained why so many high priority recruits rejected the global manufacturer's employment offer ran far deeper than their feelings of alienation in unfamiliar settings. Many harbored a deep resentment toward their parents for placing career above family. Regardless of whether or not they had been forced to move around as children, they bitterly recalled how their parents were so consumed with climbing the corporate ladder that they never really participated in their children's lives. They rarely attended school activities, were seldom home for dinner, and hardly ever made time for family outings. Instead, their parents seemed to worship at the altar of ambition.

As children, they had felt victimized by this all-consuming ambition. For them, the relentless focus on career was bad enough. When, as young adults, they watched how major corporations, rocked by a series of mergers, acquisitions, or downsizing, suddenly treated employees as an expendable commodity, they became frightened. Without warning, many of their parents had been tossed aside with little to show for a lifetime of dedication. That was the final straw.

In the Cold Light of Day

Young engineering graduates were comfortable thinking of their "career-obsessed" parents as ambitious or selfish. Seeing them as vulnerable was something entirely new and disturbing. It unnerved them. Baby Boomers had routinely worked long hours, traveled for days or weeks at a time, and, when their employer asked, canceled personal commitments at the drop of a hat. Then out of the blue, the rules of the game changed. Now as they approached retirement, instead of being rewarded for a lifetime of service, many were being laid off or forced into early retirement without the financial security they had been led to expect.

It left an indelible impression when these potential recruits witnessed how their parents, filled with anger and remorse, belatedly realized they had gotten their priorities wrong. Their parents had missed out on so many of life's important experiences. Still, the sacrifices they had made for their employers were not enough to protect their jobs or their pensions. Profoundly disillusioned and anxious about the future, Baby Boomers served as a cautionary tale for young engineering graduates determined not to make the same mistakes.

The Generational Divide

Having observed the consequences of making personal sacrifices for the sake of a career, top-tier recruits wanted none of it. Of course, when they turned down the global manufacturer's employment offer, their "answers" were couched in logical and politically correct explanations. The reason given most frequently to campus recruiters was a preference to move to Silicon Valley and join a technology company, because technology was a cutting edge industry.

Without question, technology companies were appealing, because they highly valued the critical thinking skills of these brilliant young graduates. However the same was true for the world renowned global manufacturer. Emotional-trigger research uncovered the strong emotional need of the graduates for being in a stable environment that was more in keeping with the values of their generation. They wanted jobs that left enough time to pursue personal interests that brought them pleasure and joy. They wanted to be actively involved in their children's lives rather than fritter away their children's formative years in cold impersonal hotel rooms. They wanted a real connection with their families, resisting remote assignments that relegated them to a shadowy presence. In other words they wanted—no, demanded—balance.

These talented recruits weren't lazy. They took pride in their work and wanted to excel. Some were even willing to travel extensively or work overseas. But in contrast to Baby Boomers, this generation was pragmatic and calculating. If they agreed to extensive travel or relocation abroad, it was to enhance their resume and become more marketable, not to demonstrate misguided loyalty to an employer unlikely to have their best interests at heart.

Bombarded with dire warnings of harder economic times ahead, they worried that their parents might become dependent upon them for support. Pension funds didn't guarantee the safety net they once did, the long term viability of Social Security was questionable, and the threat of terrorism was ever present. Top-tier recruits felt pressured to exercise more caution than Baby Boomers had exhibited at the beginning of their careers. They were inclined to hunker down rather than take risks. This insight took the global manufacturer by surprise. Never before had they attempted to attract a generation of engineering graduates who were more conservative than the generation that preceded them, who stubbornly put personal happiness and emotional well being above ambition and wealth.

In every conceivable way, these students represented a new breed. The company's recruitment package had never been so off the mark. As emotional-trigger research revealed, they had failed to understand what children of Baby Boomers valued. This generation cared more about relationships than money. Stability was more important than adventure. Memories outranked possessions. Happiness trumped power. The ultimate accomplishment was achieving a balanced and fulfilling life, not reaching the top rung of the corporate ladder. Attractive job offers alone did not engage them.

This posed a serious problem. As older workers started to retire, fresh talent was not lining up to take their place. Even among the small number who expressed interest, they would only consider signing on if their terms were met, and their terms were ones the global manufacturer found highly unusual. Rather than seeking more money, larger sign-on bonuses, or other typical perks, top-tier engineering candidates made quality-of-life demands.

As the manufacturer's ranks were being depleted, the time had come to revisit "their promise." They had invested considerable time and money developing what had always been a very successful employment and retention package, but precisely because of its past success, top management had difficulty envisioning a different approach. The "live and work abroad" program was so ingrained in their corporate culture, they were blinded to the fact that it no longer worked as an effective recruitment tool.

Emotional-trigger research provided a clear and definitive picture of what was important to this new wave of potential recruits, and what was not.

Emotional Trigger	What Emotional Triggers Revealed
Passions	▫ They passionately wanted to be involved in their children's lives.
Values	▫ They valued a balanced life. ▫ They valued family and leisure time more than possessions and wealth. ▫ They valued rewarding work as opposed to a high powered career. ▫ They valued long-term financial security over immediate gratification.
Feelings	▫ They felt disillusioned when they observed companies treat Baby Boomers approaching retirement as expendable commodities. ▫ They felt resentful that many of their parents had made their career their top priority.
Beliefs	▫ They believed corporate loyalty to their employees was a myth. ▫ They believed loyalty to an employer was foolish and misplaced.
Needs	▫ They needed to be anchored to a stable and nurturing community.

A Dual Career Path

Eventually, top management came to understand these puzzling young recruits. They even grew to respect them for possessing such wisdom and maturity. Emotional-trigger research helped the global manufacturer appreciate potential new recruits were neither lazy nor arrogant. Even if older executives weren't willing to admit it publicly, they grudging admired them for insisting on a balanced and meaningful life, as well as demanding the right to make their own choices. When the company realized that the recruits had no intention of delegating decision-making power over their lives to any prospective employer, the manufacturer wisely chose to accept this new reality.

Top-tier engineering graduates wanted work that was challenging and satisfying. They wanted to join a company that understood and supported their need for personal time. A company with programs in place to help them develop the skill sets needed to handle whatever challenges might come their way. They wanted supervisors who were caring and encouraging. In other words, they wanted a work life that was an extension of what their home life had been like, or, more to the point, what they wished their home life had been like. They wanted bosses who were more like parents or mentors than the traditional military models most companies followed.

Recognizing the importance of choice to new recruits, the global manufacturer overhauled their entire recruitment package. They no longer mandated only one inflexible program. Instead, they introduced a dual career path. The "live and work abroad" program was one path. Recruits who had an interest in living overseas, relocating every few years and having the opportunity to experience different cultures, could still do so. But now it was an option, not a mandate. Those who resisted were not automatically relegated to second class status within the company. There was an alternative career path that featured only one stint abroad before returning to the United States. Convinced the decision, free of consequences, was theirs to make, many top-tier candidates began to view the global manufacturer more favorably.

An entirely new set of marketing materials was created for the company's college recruiters. These materials focused on stability and quality of life, rather than the opportunity to see the world. They still included the "live and work abroad" program, because it did appeal to a number of graduates, but they made it less of a focus. Everything was overhauled to reflect the change in direction, including recruiting brochures, the Website, training materials, and the actual recruiters' sales pitch.

New messages emphasized an open culture, camaraderie of the workforce, diversity of job opportunities, the ability to work in small work team environments, and, for those to whom it held appeal, the option of living abroad. Recruits who moved overseas were no longer required to relocate every two years. The maximum number of required relocations was reduced down to three key geographic areas: the United States, Europe, and Asia or the Middle East. Potential hires who refused more than one overseas job could select the alternative program that promoted cross-discipline assignments as a second route to management opportunities.

Whether recruits worked in the United States or abroad, fresh solutions were found to ensure the ongoing transfer of knowledge between divisions. Regional marketing manager positions were created to ensure information flowed on a regular basis between local markets and the corporate headquarters. Bi-annual meetings were held for the purpose of exchanging local intelligence, collaboration, and team building.

Extensive Web-based communications were used to replace the actual experience of working abroad. Specific information on each geographic market included customs, currency, schools, traditions, work-environment data, and more. Employees were given a forum to share personal experiences.

On a smaller but equally meaningful scale, the global manufacturer implemented a number of family-friendly programs. Employees could work from home when necessary to care for a sick child. They introduced more liberal personal-time policies. Once employees qualified, they even paid for home installation of computer hook-ups.

More remote business meetings via teleconferencing were held to cut down on extended travel. Conference rooms with state-of-the-art electronics were built to facilitate such meetings. The equipment was so good, employees felt as if they were in the same room.

In order to engage this new breed of employee, the global manufacturer had to create an entirely new way of recruiting, training, and managing their workforce. Once they agreed to market their company as more than a job but as a balanced life experience, they doubled their acceptance rates within 18 months.

SUMMING UP

SELLING A COMPANY TO HIGH PRIORITY RECRUITS

Situation

A leading global manufacturer of precision tools had always been able to attract large numbers of high-caliber recruits by offering them the opportunity to live in different parts of the world. Employees were exposed to various aspects of the business through frequent transfers between divisions, often relocating with each new assignment. This approach proved an excellent strategy for sharing knowledge and reducing tensions among professionals who lacked common values, traditions, or life experiences. But as the Baby Boomer generation began to age and the talent pool changed, the company had difficulty selling their traditional incentives of travel and the opportunity to live in many parts of the world. Suddenly, acceptance rates among elite candidates plummeted. In search of insights into what motivated the younger generation, emotional-trigger research was conducted to help reverse this alarming trend.

The Potential Recruits' Emotional Triggers

Some of these candidates had already lived abroad with their parents as children and they associated the experience with feelings of isolation and social rejection. Others moved frequently within the United States and missed the lack of an anchor in their lives. More still felt deserted by their "career-obsessed" Baby Boomer parents. Rather than being free agents, they wanted jobs with plenty of leisure time to pursue personal interests and spend quality time with their own families. In other words, they demanded balance in their lives.

Genuine Insight

Having watched their parents sacrifice everything to climb the corporate ladder only to fall victim to being downsized as they approached retirement, they were profoundly disillusioned and determined not to make the same mistakes. A balanced life and a strong connection with their family and friends were their top priorities. They weren't interested in compensation alone. They wanted life experience packages. The global manufacturer realized that, for the first time, they were attempting to attract a generation of top-tier recruits who were more conservative than the generation who preceded them...who put personal happiness and emotional well being above ambition and wealth.

Solution

The relocation policy was overhauled making remote assignments a choice rather than a requirement. All policies and practices that supported the previous strategy were dismantled. New programs were put in place that guaranteed potential applicants both rewarding work and sufficient time to pursue personal interests. This holistic approach to recruitment doubled acceptance rates among top candidates within 18 months.

Part III

Putting Emotional Triggers to Work—Marketing

Chapter 8

Building the Brand

The Emotional Triggers That Launched Profitable New Ventures

A brand is your face to the world, the promise you make to your customers, your reason for being. Successful organizations treat their brand as a valuable asset, continually searching for ways to keep it rel-

> Somewhere, something incredible is waiting to be known.
> —Dr. Carl Sagan

evant and compelling. One strategy is to pursue "brand extension" opportunities by launching new products or services. This is the story about a large corporation with an established and well regarded brand that was searching for new services to offer small-business owners. Typically the company segmented small-business owners, their number-one customer group, by using traditional objective data. Although the data was factual, it wasn't how their customers saw themselves. Emotional-trigger research redefined this company's method of analyzing small-business owners and, in the process, enabled them to increase sales and successfully launch new ventures.

LESSON #5

> Regardless of how you segment them, customers are self-defining.

Leveraging a Position of Strength

A recognized industry leader had a long record of consistent growth. This company served the needs of small businesses, professional practices, and consumers in the areas of technology, electronics, consumables, office products, and furniture. Sales were strong. The time was right to leverage their position of strength. Specifically, they wanted to form strategic alliances that would enable them to offer small-business owners value-added outsourced services.

Testing Current Assumptions

Several options were already under consideration. Emotional-trigger research was used to determine if the company was on the right track or whether there were better alternatives. Small-business owners across the country participated. They represented a variety of fields including manufacturing, health, technology, marketing, insurance, professional services, personnel, distribution, engineering, and construction. The interviews were intended to provide insights into the challenges they faced and the problems that consumed disproportionate amounts of their time or sapped their mental energy.

Small-Business Owners: Five Common Challenges

It turned out that regardless of geographic location, area of specialty, or size of operation, small-business owners all contended with five critical issues. They agonized over the rising cost of providing healthcare benefits. They had great difficulty finding, motivating, and retaining qualified employees. Compliance with government regulations and IRS requirements was overwhelming. Keeping up with the rapid changes occurring within technology was exceedingly complicated. The increased speed with which they were expected to meet contractual obligations put unrealistic demands on their organizations.

Owners said their companies lacked internal resources. When they addressed morale issues, they weren't referring to employee morale; they were talking about their own. Unable to find qualified help, they were forced to scale back on their plans for growth.

They never had enough time and had trouble coping in an increasingly fast-paced environment. Two unrelated factors were the major source of the problem. Technological advances had permanently altered their customers' expectations of acceptable turnaround times needed to complete the work. At the same time that they were being pressured to work faster than ever before, they faced mounting obstacles to finding qualified personnel.

These companies were not equipped to comply with all the government and IRS regulations. They were buried in red tape and had neither the expertise nor the manpower to manage numerous human resource and payroll functions.

With the exception of technology-oriented companies that already had internal specialists, technology threw everyone else into a panic. It was changing at warp speed causing confusion and an enhanced sense of urgency. Small-business owners conceded the necessity of becoming part of the technology revolution in order to remain competitive, but had no idea how to proceed.

Similar Personal Values

Small-business owners valued continuity. In a world where they were always the little fish in a big pond, "emotional anchors" provided them with a sense of security. They placed a premium on developing long-term relationships and conducting business with the same people over time. Continuity equated to trust.

They preferred doing business with other small companies. As owners themselves, they had confidence in suppliers who were also owners, because they believed these individuals had a vested interest in providing good customer

"Many distrusted large corporations. They feared getting lost in all the bureaucracy."

service. Many distrusted large corporations. They feared getting lost in the bureaucracy. Big companies have big clients. Smaller companies, in turn, are more willing to give the time and attention equally small customers crave. Small companies equated to security and respect.

In an era of automation, these owners valued the personal approach. Whenever possible, they wanted to deal with people they knew or people who had been recommended. Familiarity equated to confidence.

Although they recognized the irony, speed was as important to small-business owners as it was to their customers. They placed a premium on quick turnaround times. If they were compelled to work faster and faster to satisfy their own customers, then they needed resources willing to help them. Responsive vendors equated to commitment and partnership.

Different Customer Profiles

Small-business owners struggled with many of the same challenges; they even shared common values. But when it came to how they actually saw themselves, the similarity ended. Categorizing them by industry, sales volume, number of employees, or geographic area proved too one-dimensional of an approach. The distinctions were more profound. What separated these owners into two groups were the stark differences between the emotional triggers that

"Small-business owners...even shared common values. But when it came to how they actually saw themselves, the similarity ended."

motivated them. Consequently, when it came to running their respective companies, they diverged sharply on attitudes about spending money.

Proprietors Versus Entrepreneurs

Proprietors comprised the first group. These individuals were focused on creating self-employment as a means of maintaining their independence. They kept their operations small and manageable. Quality personal time really mattered; they didn't want to be overwhelmed with demands that interfered with their personal interests and obligations. The business existed for the purpose of subsidizing a well-rounded life, nothing more.

Entrepreneurs made up the second customer segment. Unlike proprietors, they had ambitious goals for their companies and hoped to amass significant wealth as well as build large organizations. From the start, they had an eye toward growing their business rapidly and becoming a "major player." Characterized by a "can do" attitude, entrepreneurs exuded self-confidence. They thrived on being in charge and had great faith in their ability to orchestrate their own destiny. Their business and personal lives were inseparable, and they liked it that way.

Finding the Sweet Spot

A number of disparities separated proprietors from entrepreneurs, but there were two areas of convergence that the emotional-trigger research revealed. Exploiting the emotional triggers that united, rather than divided, proprietors and entrepreneurs represented the "sweet spot" for brand extension opportunities and provided the foundation for the strategy going forward.

The emotional triggers that defined proprietors made them prime candidates for a range of outsourced services. If the price was right, and they had confidence in the quality of the service, they'd readily embrace anything that lightened their load. The question of control never factored into the equation. As such, they were an easier target than entrepreneurs. Rather than resisting outside involvement, they wanted to lift the burden off their shoulders. Life was too short to get bogged down in time-consuming and thankless activities. However, the emotional triggers that defined and motivated entrepreneurs made them poor candidates for most outsourced services. They were leery of ceding control or trusting unknown resources to manage aspects of their business. They preferred to hire and develop their own personnel.

Emotional-trigger research revealed that entrepreneurs were open to outsourced services only when the potential threat to their business was serious enough to outweigh all other considerations. As much as they wanted to retain control, they were smart enough to recognize when it wasn't in their self-interest. Fear eclipsed self-confidence if the dread of potential consequences overshadowed their inclination to reject external "interference." Yet only when confronted by such circumstances did the predominant emotional trigger influencing their behavior switch from "authority" to "survival."

From the entrepreneur's perspective only two issues qualified. Complying with countless IRS payroll and employee regulations was akin to navigating alien territory laced with landmines. Equally fraught with peril were the mysteries of technology. Either issue, if mismanaged, could severely wound their operation; if both were mismanaged the outcome would be lethal. Identifying the hierarchy of emotional triggers shared by proprietors and entrepreneurs made it possible to exploit these two "consensus issues."

Proprietors and entrepreneurs had very different self-images. They wanted different things from their businesses and they had very different priorities about how they chose to operate their companies. Emotional-trigger research clarified those differences and helped to prioritize the few instances when their self-interests overlapped. Page 129 shows the emotional triggers that formed the "sweet spot" around which proprietors and entrepreneurs converged.

EMOTIONAL TRIGGER	WHAT EMOTIONAL TRIGGERS REVEALED
Feelings	▫ They felt intimidated by all the government and IRS regulations. ▫ They felt threatened by technology advancements and insecure about their ability to navigate change. ▫ They felt vulnerable because they lacked affordable resources to help them deal with government and technology issues.
Needs	▫ They needed to feel valued; not like a small fish in a big pond.
Beliefs	▫ They believed their interests would be best served by working with other small-business owners or companies that catered exclusively to small businesses.
Experiences	▫ They experienced limited choices from service providers disinterested in small accounts.

Exploiting the Sweet Spot: Profitable New Ventures

The first "consensus issue" was the need to ensure ongoing compliance with government payroll tax and employment requirements.

In response, a strategic alliance was formed with a payroll accounting firm. The industry leader leveraged the combined revenue potential of their extensive customer base and negotiated a lower fee structure than any of the business owners could have obtained themselves. Everyone benefited from the arrangement. Small-business owners were able to receive expert services for a fee that wasn't available to them individually. The company increased sales among their key customer segment by using the insights the emotional-trigger research provided to further engage small-business owners.

Sensitive to their customers' need to avoid feeling like a small fish in a big pond, they selected a strategic partner whose niche was serving small and mid-sized companies. The choice of this strategic partner reinforced the small-business owners' need for respect and security. If the majority of other customers were also small owners, they felt reassured. The company came out ahead by identifying a timely and profitable brand extension opportunity. At the same time, they reinforced their leadership position among small-business owners as a value-added partner.

The second "consensus issue" was technology. Recognizing the lack of services available to small-business owners, the company developed a multi-pronged solution. Strategic alliances were formed with technology experts who helped with hardware and software decisions, integration, and related issues. Alliances were formed with service providers at the back end to handle maintenance and repair. For quick and low cost assistance, online support functions were enhanced.

Both the payroll and technology brand extensions were a natural outgrowth of the industry leader's core competencies. Each strategic alliance offered upside revenue potential without requiring upfront investments as the cost of entry. The company achieved their objective of launching successful brand extensions and, in the process, they strengthened relationships with high-priority customers.

SUMMING UP
BUILDING THE BRAND

Situation

An industry leader serving the technology, electronics, consumables, office products, and furniture needs of small businesses, professional practices, and consumers wanted to explore strategic alliances that would enable them to offer new outsourced services to small-business owners, their most important customer segment. Emotional-trigger research was used to provide insights into the challenges small-business owners faced and the problems that consumed their time, in order to identify the most viable brand extension opportunities. It soon became apparent that while small-business owners shared common personal values, they diverged sharply when it came to running their companies. These owners fell into two distinct groups: proprietors and entrepreneurs. The first group viewed their business as a means of subsidizing a well-rounded life. They didn't want to be overwhelmed by demands that infringed on their personal time and welcomed outside assistance. Entrepreneurs, on the other hand, had ambitious goals for amassing wealth and building large organizations. Their businesses and personal lives were intertwined. Characterized by a "can do" attitude, they were leery of relinquishing control, preferring instead to hire and develop internal talent.

Small-Business Owners' Emotional Triggers

They felt intimidated by government and IRS regulations. They were threatened by technology advancements. They felt particularly vulnerable because they lacked the ability to adequately deal with either.

Genuine Insight

Typically, small-business owners were segmented in traditional ways on the basis of industry, size, or geographic location. Although the data was factual, it wasn't how they saw themselves. Emotional-trigger research identified stark differences between "proprietors" and "entrepreneurs." Proprietors were interested in a broad range of support services, anything to lighten their load. That wasn't the case with entrepreneurs. Only when fear overshadowed their need for control were they open to outside assistance. And only two things frightened entrepreneurs: compliance with government regulations and technology.

Solution

By changing the method of analyzing their customers, this industry leader was able to identify, prioritize, and launch profitable new brand extensions guaranteed to have the broadest appeal. Initiatives included a strategic alliance with a payroll accounting firm that catered to the needs of small companies and partnerships with technology experts who offered front end support as well as back-end maintenance and repair.

Chapter 9

Co-existing With the Industry Giant

The Emotional Triggers That Repositioned a Service Business

Some changes occur gradually. At other times, the competitive landscape is rocked by a seismic shift. This is the story of a mid-sized independent moving company that found themselves in such a situation.

> If you only look at what is, you might never attain what could be.
> —Anonymous

When an industry giant introduced a revolutionary new way of doing business, it threatened this mid-sized company's very survival. Emotional-trigger research provided the framework that enabled them to compete.

LESSON #6

> Don't be intimidated. Bigger isn't always better.

The Times, They Were A-Changin'

There was a time, in the not too distant past, when small and mid-sized businesses could thrive on the basis of providing superior customer service, but that was before external factors outside their control sparked a paradigm shift. Large corporations, often their major customers, came under mounting pressure from shareholders and their board of directors to contain costs, frequently at the expense of other considerations. Their requirements became more demanding and more sophisticated. Lacking both the resources and the expertise to accommodate this new dynamic, it became harder and harder for many small businesses to remain competitive.

In one industry after another, from banking to steel, consolidators saw an opportunity to swoop in and transform the way business was conducted by promising large corporations the ability to better leverage their expenses. When it happened within the relocation industry, a second-generation moving company known for their personalized service became the latest victim of this sad but all too familiar tale. Seemingly overnight, they went from a thriving local business that enjoyed long-term contractual agreements with a number of major corporations to a company struggling for its very existence.

Up to now, this mid-sized moving company had successfully competed against larger chains by establishing close personal relationships with their clients. They worked directly with the corporate employee responsible for relocation and, through the years, had gained the trust of these individuals. On the strength of the personal relationships they had cultivated, their company had grown and prospered. But times were changing rapidly and the old ways of conducting business no longer guaranteed future success. As change swirled around them, their approach to the business had not kept pace. Their systems were antiquated, and they were behind the curve when it came to using cutting-edge technology or innovative new marketing strategies. That made them extremely vulnerable to a predatory competitor, who was rethinking their entire industry.

David Versus Goliath

Although this mid-sized moving company continued to conduct business as usual, a major consolidator, busy redefining the overall business model, loomed on the **"They intended to transform the industry from a fragmented group of small, independent, service providers to a consolidated, national service business."** horizon. First, the consolidator acquired several established real estate companies. Then using those acquisitions as a springboard, they set out to become the country's preeminent turnkey relocation resource. Not only would they provide moving services, but they would also assist employees to secure a mortgage, sell an existing home, and purchase a new home. They intended to transform the industry from a fragmented group of small, independent, service providers to a consolidated, national service business that handled every aspect of a corporation's relocation requirements.

From the consolidator's vantage point, the timing couldn't have been better. Corporations were looking to cut back on non-essential internal support functions. Unfortunately, this mid-sized moving company had concentrated their efforts on forging relationships with lower-level relocation specialists, the very people most likely to lose their jobs. Focusing instead on the decision-makers, the consolidator plunged into the "power vacuum." They met with senior human resource officers and promised to save them money on every aspect of employee relocation, from the cost of moving services to all the related real-estate transactions. Then they went a step further and convinced human resource executives to outsource the entire process. They guaranteed corporations they'd be able to reduce staff, free themselves of time-consuming tasks, and, most significantly, reduce their cost per move.

Eager to find relatively painless ways to reduce their overhead expense, many large corporations quickly embraced this new concept. Within record time, the internal relocation-specialist positions had been eliminated, and the consolidator was responsible for awarding business to all the suppliers who had previously worked directly with corporate personnel.

The mid-sized moving company had been completely squeezed out of the picture. In the blink of an eye, they had lost all their major clients to this menacing new "employer." Soon the consolidator became a powerful gatekeeper that dictated all the terms under which they would employ local moving companies. In exchange for future business referrals, they not only demanded a commission, but pressed the moving company for bigger and bigger fee concessions. The cost reductions that came out of the mid-sized moving company's profits were then split between the consolidator and their corporate accounts.

Dazed and floundering, this mid-sized moving company had no idea how to co-exist with a consolidator who combined time saving state-of-the-art technology with guaranteed cost reductions at their expense. When the situation became untenable and threatened to put them out of business, they turned to emotional-trigger research to find a solution.

The Courtship

From the start, when the consolidator first met with senior human resource executives to introduce their service, they were greeted with considerable interest and enthusiasm. Managing employee relocations was a difficult, emotionally draining, and labor-intensive job that was not a core competency for these

"It was a perfect fit. Or so it seemed at the time."

companies. Under pressure to reduce overhead costs and become more efficient, executives were quick to embrace outsourcing the entire process to a national, turnkey relocation resource. It was a perfect fit. Or so it seemed at the time.

One large corporation after another jumped on the bandwagon. There were many apparent advantages, while the downside appeared negligible. First and foremost, they would reduce their cost per move. The promise of exceptional service was enticing, and it was very reassuring to be guaranteed round-the-clock hand-holding by an extensive team of experts drawn from their partner's very own real-estate companies. The consolidator had convinced senior executives they were being presented with a win-win opportunity. Human resource departments would gain a resource with the experience and commitment to better manage employee relocations. They'd be able to reduce expenses, cut headcount, and get rid of a myriad of thankless administrative tasks. Why would anyone hesitate to sign up? Well, as it turned out, very few did.

As the consolidator pressed their case, skillfully elaborating on all the advantages they offered, how could anyone not be tantalized? They promised accurate and timely processing of all claims. They promised significant cost savings per move. They promised enhanced capacity because of the depth, breadth, and reach of their expertise. They promised unparalleled service. And, with heartwarming sincerity, they promised to handle each and every one of the corporations' employees with great empathy and care.

So, after such a masterful courtship, when the consolidator finally "popped the question," corporations responded with a resounding "yes," most without so much as a backward glance.

The Honeymoon

Initially, as with most honeymoons, the relationship began on a positive note. Confident they had chosen the right partner, senior human resource executives outsourced their entire relocation operation to the consolidator. Relinquishing the reins of control was liberating. They had freed themselves of a thankless job *and* gained a team of professionals with far more resources and expertise than previously existed within their own internal departments. It was a heady time characterized by optimism, trust, and high expectations.

At first, their trust and optimism seemed justified. No one even entertained the notion it may have been misplaced. After all, the consolidator had quickly honored their promise to reduce the cost-per-employee move. In addition to delivering significant savings, they made it possible for large corporations to reduce the number of full-time employees on their payroll.

Oblivious to the strong-arm tactics being used to accomplish these objectives or the potential longer-term conse-

> **"If it came with a hidden cost, the cost had not yet been discovered."**

quences of such tactics, human resource executives basked in the kudos that came their way from top management. At a time when large corporations were being hammered by shareholders and their boards of directors to streamline operations, aligning with this relocation consolidator was being hailed as a smart and innovative decision. If it came with a hidden cost, the cost had not yet been discovered.

Instead of being required to manage countless numbers of independent vendors around the country, human resource executives liked having only one point of contact. Corporations were happy. The consolidator was certainly happy. Everyone benefited from this new arrangement, with the obvious exception of the mid-sized moving company.

Marriage: The Reality Check

By the time emotional-trigger research was conducted with senior human resource executives, the turnkey relocation partnership had been in place for several years, and the bloom was off the rose. The honeymoon and all the hopes that went with it had faded to a distant memory. In the cold light of day, this arrangement was seen through an entirely different prism. Problems were surfacing everywhere. Rather than being the beneficiary of the consolidator's services, human resource executives now felt hostage to a marriage that wasn't working.

The consolidator's rate of growth was outpacing their ability to deliver services as promised. Plagued by constant staff turnover, details routinely fell through the cracks. Having already eliminated their own relocation staff, the consolidator's failure to meet contractual obligations left human resource executives with nowhere to turn. Large corporations found they were saddled with as much work as they had before they ever outsourced their relocation operation. The type of work may have changed, but not the volume. On top of everything else, they had to constantly retrain new staff assigned to their account on their company's policies and procedures. There was no continuity.

At least their in-house staff had been stable. Human resource executives regretted what, in retrospect, now seemed like a hasty decision. Yes, they had saved the cost of a few in-house employees, but at what price? The original hassles they sought to eliminate now paled in comparison to what they were forced to confront. When the decision was made to utilize the turnkey relocation service in place of in-house staff, senior human resource executives assigned oversight of the function to someone else within their department. It was originally assumed these individuals, none of whom had relocation experience, would simply pass along general information and the consolidator would take it from there. But as problem after problem arose with the consolidator, these human resource employees were forced to take a more active role, and they were overwhelmed.

Regret

Senior human resource executives felt betrayed by the consolidator, but they were equally upset with themselves. Many felt they had been too trusting. Without hesitation, they had tossed aside long-term relationships with the local, mid-sized moving company for an unknown. Under the best of circumstances, employee relocations were emotional for those uprooting their lives and those of their families. But the mid-sized moving company, with their exceptional level of service, could always be relied upon to make the actual move as stress free as possible. It was a bitter irony that the cost savings realized from eliminating a few staff jobs and outsourcing the relocation operation resulted in actually demoralizing employees in the midst of moving, at the very time when it was most important to maintain their spirits. The cost of cost reductions was too high!

Had they been fair? Had they been wise? Or, had they been careless? These were the questions senior human resource executives were asking themselves. They hadn't anticipated their congenial relationship with the local moving company would become strained, because the consolidator was demanding the same level of service at considerably lower rates. The local mover was no longer willing or able to extend themselves. Employees were caught in the middle. They were increasingly unhappy about how their moves were being handled, and it was reflected in their work performance. That was the last thing human resource departments wanted.

Relocations were supposed to ensure happy transitions for valued employees. Realizing that just the opposite was happening, many senior human resource executives lamented how they had gotten their priorities so wrong. They had bought into the consolidator's emphasis on profit potential and staff reductions to the exclusion of everything else. Now that it may be too late, they realized it did little good to receive rebates on every move if job performance suffered because of poor employee morale. They were struck with buyer's remorse.

Now What?

Regardless of how unhappy senior human resource executives were with the consolidator, they were boxed into a situation of their own making. Having already been publicly praised for contributing significant cost savings to the bottom line, they were in no position to return to management, hat in hand, to request more money. There was no putting the genie back in the bottle. Some executives worried their credibility and influence with top management would be diminished and wanted to save face, regardless of the consequences. Others, even more concerned, feared their mistake might cost them their job. They desperately wanted to return to the service levels the local mover had provided before the consolidator ruthlessly decimated their profits and incentive. But how? They had run out of options.

Emotional-trigger research uncovered the extent to which senior human resource executives were driven by two emotional triggers: their fear of admitting their mistakes publicly and their sense of powerlessness to undo a bad situation.

EMOTIONAL TRIGGER	WHAT EMOTIONAL TRIGGERS REVEALED
Feelings	▣ They felt betrayed and deceived when the consolidator failed to deliver the level of service promised. ▣ They felt embarrassed and insecure about admitting their error in judgment to top management. ▣ They felt trapped in a poor decision of their own making. ▣ They felt angry and impotent at having lost control and options. ▣ They felt reduced to hoping for an elusive solution.
Experience	▣ Lacking in-house resources, they experienced a sense of helplessness.

A One-Two Punch

Emotional-trigger research made it clear that many senior human resource executives wished they had never formed an alliance with the turnkey relocation company. They were eager to undo the damage that had been done, but they didn't know how. Powerless to alter the relationship if, bottom line, the cost per move increased, they were a dispirited group.

Although human resource executives and the local moving company had each lost ground, they shared a common objective. Both wanted to reconnect with one another. But the rules of the game for these large corporations, as well as the service providers they had previously employed, had been inextricably altered. Fortunately, the insights uncovered through emotional-trigger research revealed how their interests converged.

Human resource executives needed to improve employee morale by offering a relocation package that, once again, included first-rate, personalized service. The local mover needed, once again, to make a reasonable profit. Neither was in a position to eliminate the consolidator, but they could join forces and, by presenting a united front, deliver a one-two punch to their nemesis.

First, the mid-size moving company needed to change their business model. Remaining competitive in the corporate relocation business required forming a strategic association with a nationally recognized partner. Reclaiming their fair share of the long haul relocation business began with the recognition that this mid-sized moving company was only one of many local movers being squeezed by the consolidator within their market. They had to close ranks to gain leverage.

The solution was to form an association and then reach out collectively to a major national moving organization that had the resources, expertise, and "muscle" to compete with the consolidator. And that's what they did. Under this arrangement, local movers paid a fee to affiliate with a leading national moving company and, in exchange, the national organization favorably renegotiated terms with the local consolidator. Buttressed by their newfound strength, the mid-sized moving company circumvented the consolidator and met directly with their former corporate accounts. They emphasized the superior level of customer service they had always provided but, in more recent years, had been undermined by the consolidator's greed.

Senior human resource executives weren't going to make the same mistake twice. This time around, they established their own list of approved moving companies. Then they demanded the consolidator only hire movers from that list. The pressure applied by senior human resource executives, combined with the clout the mid-sized company acquired through affiliation with a national moving organization, provided the ammunition to deliver that long awaited one-two punch. The consolidator was forced to renegotiate its fees and reduce their demands.

The very act of organizing put the consolidator on notice that they had overplayed their hand. Commissions to the local mover increased. Employees being relocated were treated with the care and attention they deserved. Human resource executives reclaimed a measure of control by improving the customer service they received without incurring additional expenditures. At last, the moving company was able to successfully insulate themselves against the consolidator's strong-arm tactics. For the first time in years, business was booming.

Emotional-trigger research provided the customer insights this mid-sized moving company needed to create a successful new business model that served both their interests and those of their former customers. They learned that bigger isn't always better. And human resource executives, much to their chagrin, learned that too.

SUMMING UP
CO-EXISTING WITH THE INDUSTRY GIANT

Situation

A mid-sized moving company known for personalized service was shocked when many of their long-standing, corporate customers suddenly signed with a new organization. This new organization, positioned as the "resident relocation expert," offered a revolutionary turnkey relocation package that not only included moving services but assistance with securing a mortgage and purchasing a new home. They promised companies would be able to reduce staff, outsource time-consuming administrative tasks, and, most significantly, reduce the cost per move. Soon they became a powerful gatekeeper that dictated all the terms under which they would employ local moving companies. In exchange for future business referrals, they demanded fee reductions as well as a commission. With their long term survival at risk, the moving company turned to emotional-trigger research to help develop a competitive strategy.

The Clients' Emotional Triggers

Many former corporate customers felt betrayed, because the turnkey consolidator had failed to deliver on their initial promises. Left to cope with inadequate services, the problem was now exacerbated by a lack of in-house resources. They were angry at having lost control and some feared losing their jobs. Reduced to merely hoping service levels would improve, they felt helpless.

Genuine Insight

Because the promised cost savings had already been realized, corporate executives were resigned to keeping the program in place, but they lamented the loss of valuable personalized attention. They desperately sought a way to maintain cost savings, reinstate the former levels of service, and save face within their own organizations.

Solution

The solution was to reinvent the mid-sized company's business model by forging an association with a national moving organization that had the resources, expertise, and "muscle" to compete with the consolidator. In exchange for paying to affiliate, the arrangement with the consolidator was favorably renegotiated. Buttressed by their newfound strength, the mid-sized company circumvented the consolidator and met directly with their former corporate accounts. They emphasized the superior level of customer service they had always provided. Senior human resource executives, determined not to make the same mistake twice, demanded the consolidator only use movers on their approved list. The combined pressure from corporate clients and the national moving company they had affiliated with delivered a one-two punch and forced the consolidator to renegotiate fees. The moving company was able to successfully insulate their company against the consolidator's strong-arm tactics. For the first time in years, business was better than ever.

Chapter 10

Inventing a New Business

The Emotional Triggers That Turned a Popular Activity Into a National Industry

What happens when a new business idea becomes so successful that the very people who helped you launch it and know every aspect of the operation inside-out suddenly are

> Every path to a new understanding begins in confusion.
> —Mason Cooley

among your fiercest competition? That's exactly what happened when the owner of a regional gym chain capitalized on a grassroots interest in cheerleading. He repositioned his business as a major tournament organizer and joined forces with other industry leaders. Then former employees, eager to replicate the business model, opened independent gyms and began to sponsor competitions of their own. As these competitions mushroomed, they started to eat away at the tournament organizer's customer base. This is the story of how emotional-trigger research led to an innovative strategic solution.

LESSON #7

If the competition threatens your market share, redefine your market.

Rah, Rah! Sis, Boom, Bah!

For decades, a Southwest-based, gym-chain owner had profited from a widespread interest in cheerleading. His gyms gave young people the opportunity to develop cheerleading skills outside of school by providing them with a special place to learn and practice. At first, his focus was exclusively on professional instruction. Before long, recognizing the natural inclination of athletes is to compete, he diversified by organizing local, then regional, and, finally, national competitions. Soon the competitions eclipsed professional instruction as his primary business.

The events caught on quickly and became enormously popular. Parents embraced a positive alternative for children who wanted to be cheerleaders without having to endure the indignity of high school popularity contests. Young people gained a newfound self-esteem. It wasn't necessary to be part of the "in" crowd to join the gym, learn a skill, or go on to compete locally, perhaps even nationally. Everyone had an opportunity to experience some of the same satisfaction and prestige that "popular" kids did.

Parents, keen to support their children's dream, represented a lucrative market waiting to be tapped. Regional and national tournaments offered multiple new revenue streams that far surpassed the potential of neighborhood gyms. The tournament organizer opened summer cheerleading camps, charged fees for event participation, sold admission tickets, branched out into uniform sales, and received commissions on all related concession enterprises. Everyone was happy. The organizer's business was growing by leaps and bounds. Young people, thrilled to be cheerleaders complete with uniforms, ribbons, and trophies, found acceptance as part of a new community of friends. Parents were pleased to see their children succeed at something they loved.

There was only one problem: the competitions were not legitimate. So the tournament organizer, determined to rectify the problem, launched a campaign to elevate cheerleading to a nationally accredited sport. He joined forces with the other major event owners and sponsors around the country who dominated this small but growing industry. Together, they established uniform standards and created a national organization to ensure that the tournaments were officially sanctioned. Rules and regulations were adopted regarding what constituted an acceptable performance, how many contests were permissible, and the authorized levels of participation. All the pieces appeared to be in place.

But appearances can be deceiving. Establishing uniform standards proved to be a two-edged sword. Although it *did* guarantee that a win would be sanctioned as legitimate, it also reduced the number of opportunities to win. The upshot was that as cheerleading edged closer to being a nationally accredited sport, two groups with conflicting priorities emerged. Those who valued recognition over exclusivity found themselves at odds.

Too Much of a Good Thing

Some parents, accustomed to having their child win, did not welcome new rules and more stringent regulations. They resisted the drive for creating a nationally accredited sport if it came at the expense of their child's ego gratification. At the same time this struggle was unfolding, the confluence of two other factors occurred that dramatically changed the marketplace dynamics. Smaller groups of gyms were forced to consolidate in order to gain a more powerful voice. Simultaneously, larger cheerleading companies, seeking to establish dominance in this burgeoning industry, either merged with their rivals or acquired them. The dual consolidation left many employees without jobs.

A number of former employees, well aware that "winning" often fueled a parent's willingness to pay considerable sums of money for their child to participate, wanted to cash in on this profitable and rapidly growing new industry. In record numbers, employees who had been laid off joined by many others who had chosen to resign, opened cheerleading gyms. They were already intimately familiar with how cheerleading companies made their money, and they were confident of their ability to leverage this knowledge. The business had no certification requirements, the cost of entry was low, and it demanded little or no training. It had all the earmarks of an attractive low-risk proposition with a large built-in pool of customers who would generously "ante up" for their child to learn new skills.

From the start, these new gym owners launched their own local and regional cheerleading competitions. Sponsoring these events generated additional revenue and provided their members with more opportunities to "win." For a time, the strategy was effective. It brought new members to their gyms and helped them retain existing ones. Eventually, the inevitable happened. Independent gym owners had flooded the market with competitions. It was too much of a good thing. Large and small event organizers alike experienced an erosion of business. But the fledgling entrepreneurs, lacking management expertise and not knowing how else to proceed, continued on their self-destructive course.

No Way to Fight It, No Way to Win

The desire for recognition had finally collided with the desire for exclusivity. As the number of competitions exploded, major event organizers and

> **"Rather than achieving their aim of a nationally accredited sport, the industry was splintering before their eyes."**

sponsors saw a decline in interest. Rather than becoming a nationally accredited sport, the industry was splintering before their eyes. Even parents who had previously supported the influx of more competitive venues became disgruntled. Everyone seemed to be sponsoring a competition. A child might win first place in one event, only to have a friend win first place in an event sponsored by a different gym across town. Ribbons and trophies became increasingly meaningless. The sheer volume of cheerleading events undermined any sense of legitimacy. Contestants felt robbed of the opportunity to ever be recognized as "best in class."

This presented an ominous threat to the major tournament organizer. Although he was embroiled in a difficult effort to standardize and accredit cheerleading as a national sport, his business was thrust into a battle for survival. Competitions were losing credibility, his customer base was shrinking, and profits were being eroded. He was deeply upset with former employees who were destroying the business. Battling feelings of betrayal, he vacillated between wanting to crush them, plotting to acquire them, or figuring out how to work with them.

In Chapter 9, we shared the story of a mid-sized moving company in danger of being squeezed out of business by a giant consolidator. In this instance, the tournament organizer confronted the opposite problem. Now it was the giant under siege. The encroachment of small independent gyms, each hosting their own competitions, was severely jeopardizing the future of his business. Former employees had stolen "trade secrets" and over-saturated the market. The industry was riddled with confusion. Dreams of national accreditation were fading.

The tournament organizer was confounded by new gym owners. What could they possibly be thinking? What was driving them? And more importantly, what should he do about it? Somehow he had to block them from hosting their own competitions, while maintaining their goodwill. It was a delicate balancing act, but it was a necessary one if they were ever to support his goal of a nationally accredited sport. In frustration, the tournament organizer turned to emotional-trigger research to find a strategic solution.

The Cheer Had Gone Out of Cheerleading

Many former employees, now independent gym owners, realized they had bitten off more than they could chew. They never intended to pit themselves against the major tournament

"All they wanted was a small piece of this new industry. They assumed the opportunities were limitless."

organizers. Nor was it their intention to damage or diminish anyone's business. All they wanted was a small piece of this dynamic new industry. They assumed the opportunities were limitless. Unfortunately, they never realized, until it was too late, how so many different competitions would overwhelm the marketplace. Like it or not, they were boxed into a corner. Their own competitions were suffering. Worse yet, they had inadvertently alienated their former employers and the industry's major tournament organizers. For them, the cheer had definitely gone out of cheerleading.

Sponsoring competitions was not even the priority for new gym owners. They were simply looking for ways to improve profits, and hosting tournaments seemed like a logical move. There was never any animosity involved, only a desire to make more money. Now they found themselves in an impossible situation. Admittedly, they were no match for the major tournament organizers, but they had invested their life savings in their gyms and had to survive.

From the beginning, emotional-trigger research exposed a disconnect between what the Southwest-based tournament organizer presumed and what was really motivating former employees. New gym owners had sincerely believed there was plenty of business to go around. As small independent operators, they never imagined they would be seen as "the competition." The predicament left them worried and feeling extremely vulnerable. Although they understood cheerleading and knew how to attract and train new customers, many were struggling to manage other aspects of their operation. They lacked experience running a business and were unprepared for the day-to-day problems of managing cash flow, promoting their gym, or effectively competing against neighboring facilities. They had no idea how to develop a marketing plan or run a budget. A great many were under funded. The fear of losing their business was a constant. Rather than finding security in being their own boss, they felt unprotected and in over their heads.

Give Us Some H-E-L-P!

What initially seemed like a sure-fire business proposition had turned into something more daunting. Accustomed to a steady stream of customers attracted to the major organizers' tournaments, these new gym owners had no idea what to do when demand for their own events dried up. Matters were further complicated, because sponsoring cheerleading tournaments was a fairly new industry. Many of the established processes that typically help keep a business on track were missing.

In this mom-and-pop environment, new owners did not always have sufficient, well-trained staff, adequate systems and procedures, or established customer-service policies. Communications were infrequent and inconsistent. They were at a loss, without one reliable source for gathering timely information about all upcoming events. As these gym owners let down their guard and spoke about their experiences, they made a startling admission. It was an admission that stunned the tournament organizer and was to have far-reaching implications. They needed help. They longed for a support system.

Contrary to the organizer's previous assumptions, independent gym owners conceded the folly of continuing to sponsor their own events. They knew professionally managed competitions that were well-organized, began on schedule, had respected judges, and were deemed safe were more important to attracting customers—and to protecting their revenue stream—than managing their own local tournaments. If these elements could be guaranteed, they were confident they'd be more successful. But as long as cheerleading events continued to inundate the market, disillusioned customers would not consider them legitimate.

Emotional-trigger research provided the tournament organizer with a more sympathetic view of independent-gym owners. Once he saw them as vulnerable, rather than predatory, he was able to get past his anger and arrive at a mutually beneficial solution.

EMOTIONAL TRIGGER	WHAT EMOTIONAL TRIGGERS REVEALED
Experiences	▫ They experienced difficulties managing their day-to-day business operations, leaving them insecure and prone to making poor decisions out of desperation. ▫ They experienced a steady erosion of their business as customers grew disillusioned with too many different competitions.
Feelings	▫ Having angered major tournament organizers, they felt vulnerable and were afraid of how they might retaliate. ▫ They felt that they could not adequately address the competitive challenges that overwhelmed them and feared their business would fail. ▫ They felt terrified that they had invested their life's savings and might lose everything.

United We Stand

New gym owners were interested in a program that supported their business goals, offered much-needed training, and provided operational expertise. They were more emotionally invested in finding help, than in hosting their own local competitions. Driven by a need to be rescued, their dominant emotional triggers were a sense of vulnerability, inadequacy, and fear. Once these triggers were exposed, the solution was obvious. It turned out to be a mirror image of the one presented in Chapter 9. The mid-size moving company affiliated with a national organization to protect itself from the predatory practices of the industry's leading consolidator.

Although the tables were reversed, an affiliate program proved to be the answer for the major tournament organizer as well. Coming at it from the opposite perspective, his plans for elevating cheerleading to a nationally accredited sport had been thrown into disarray. He desperately needed to blunt the encroachment of small-gym owners, who had created a chaotic marketplace and were draining his profit base. Emotional-trigger research pointed him in the right direction. Draconian measures were unnecessary. He didn't have to quash the competition or scheme to acquire them for pennies on the dollar. New gym owners were joiners, not fighters. They could be united under one umbrella that would both advance the national accreditation objective *and* represent a new source of income.

Small-gym owners welcomed the idea of an affiliation with peers that would provide an opportunity to exchange knowledge and to socialize. They were willing to pay a reasonable fee in exchange for access to essential practices and operating systems. They wanted the ability to participate in co-op advertising programs, and they immediately saw the benefit of leveraging their purchasing power to get better deals on everything from supplies to computers, telephone service, and office equipment. Locking these gym owners into a mutually dependent relationship gave the tournament organizer a network of gyms committed to supporting his need for standardization. Armed with that insight, he was determined to craft an affiliate program that was more valuable to independent gyms than the opportunity to host their own local events.

He hosted regional meetings to outline the affiliate program and gage the level of interest. Care was taken to provide adequate time for reviewing the program and holding open discussions. No longer concerned that independent gym owners were the "enemy," the major tournament organizer listened carefully to what they needed and structured the affiliate program accordingly. In exchange for the advantages of affiliation, gym owners agreed to comply with standardized industry regulations. As both relief and excitement grew, affiliates sought to become the new gold standard for industry performance.

Emotional-trigger research helped the tournament organizer dissect and diffuse a complex problem. It enabled him to empathize with his competition, because, for the first time, he saw the challenge through their emotional prism. The insights he gained taught him a valuable lesson: if the competition threatens your market share, redefine your market. And that's exactly what he did. To everyone's benefit, he was well on his way to establishing cheerleading as a nationally accredited sport.

SUMMING UP
INVENTING A NEW BUSINESS

Situation

For decades, the owner of a Southwest-based gym had capitalized on a grassroots interest in cheerleading. At first, he focused exclusively on instruction. However, recognizing that the natural inclination of athletes is to compete, he soon repositioned his business and became a major tournament organizer. He joined forces with other tournament organizers and developed new revenue streams, including summer cheerleading camps, uniform sales, event participation fees, entrance fees, concessions, and advertising commissions. As interest in these competitions grew, his business was hugely successful. But a problem developed: the competitions weren't legitimate. So he launched a campaign to establish cheerleading as a nationally accredited sport. Along with the other major event organizers who dominated this small, but growing, industry, he established uniform standards and created a national organization to ensure that the tournaments were officially sanctioned. All the pieces seemed to be in place. Then the industry consolidated and many employees lost their jobs. These former employees, eager to replicate the business model they had observed firsthand, opened independent cheerleading gyms and began to sponsor competitions of their own. Soon the market was flooded with so many events, customers grew disillusioned and participation declined. The Southwest-based organizer watched with alarm as his profits and customer base eroded. Not knowing whether to crush, acquire, or seek to work with the new gym owners who were threatening his business, he turned to emotional-trigger research to find a strategic solution.

The Small-Gym Owners' Emotional Triggers

Independent, small-gym owners, eager to cash in on this rapidly growing industry, thought they had invested in a low risk venture. It didn't turn out that way. As the market became saturated, they were afraid of losing their life's savings and terrified that the major organizers wanted to destroy them. They felt vulnerable and unprotected. With little or no management experience, they felt inadequately prepared to manage their business in a volatile environment.

Genuine Insight

New gym owners were focused exclusively on maximizing their sources of revenue. They never intended to compete with their former employers. What they really wanted was a mutually beneficial working relationship. They just didn't know how to accomplish their goal.

Solution

The Southwest-based organizer established an affiliate program. Under this arrangement, local gyms benefited from best practices and operating systems, leveraged their purchasing power, and participated in co-op advertising campaigns. In exchange, they agreed to comply with standardized industry regulations and refrained from hosting competing tournaments. The organizer regained customers, profits increased, and he created a lucrative new revenue stream.

Chapter 11

Marketing to Donors

The Emotional Triggers That Increased Contributions

Everyone wants our money, and it's increasingly difficult to choose between so many worthy causes. That's why countless institutions

> There is a craft and a power in listening.
> —Glenn Gould

and organizations are struggling. Endeavoring to break through the clutter, one small, but highly respected, liberal-arts college tried to engage new donors by organizing alumni events and sharing regular updates about campus activities, through a variety of different venues. Efforts focused on requests for support of ongoing operational expenses or broad new initiatives. This is the story of how emotional-trigger research helped this institution humanize their approach and engage more potential donors.

LESSON #8

> Humanizing the pitch touches the heart and opens the wallet.

Please Sir, May We Have Some More?

This well regarded, but modestly endowed, liberal-arts college was in the process of developing their fundraising strategy for an upcoming multi-year campaign. They had set an ambitious goal for themselves, seeking to double the total contributions received during their previous initiative. Everyone charged with accomplishing this goal recognized the institution was at a crossroad. Incorporating proven strategies from the past was an important first step, but it wasn't enough. The success of future endeavors required the cultivation of a more comprehensive pipeline of new donors. Rather than continuing to rely on a small group of wealthy individuals, the college had to inoculate itself, in the event that pledges made by any of these individuals failed to materialize.

A Different Breed

The college's development officers had established relationships with alumni who were now senior citizens, as well as with the older Baby Boomers, who had graduated in the late 1960s and 1970s. But younger Baby Boomers, who came of age in the early 1980s, were another matter. Actually, they were a complete mystery. Historically, development officers had kept alumni involved with their alma mater by ensuring they remained "in the loop." Efforts included planning reunions, working with local alumni chapters to schedule events and social activities, e-mail solicitations, sending out letters from the president, periodic college updates, and publishing a first rate alumni magazine. These tactics, so effective with previous generations, repeatedly failed to produce similar results among younger Baby Boomers.

Now, for the first time, many of these younger Baby Boomers had the income and financial resources to make a significant contribution to the college. Unfortunately, very little was known about their attitudes, beliefs, aspirations, and behavior. If the college was to have any success tapping into this potentially lucrative but elusive donor pool, they first had to understand who these alumni were, what they really valued, and how best to engage them. Senior officers and the board of trustees commissioned emotional-trigger research to provide these crucial insights.

Clash of the Boomers

Although younger Baby Boomers shared the same "Baby Boomer" label with graduates of the previous decade, it turned out they shared little else. Unlike their older counterparts who grew up during the turbulent 1960s, these alumni came of age during a period of relative calm and stability. Their formative years were not shaped by the upheaval that spawned a generation who railed against convention and wanted to change the world. In fact they completely rejected this approach to life. Instead, they were more pragmatic and conservative. They didn't want to change the world. They just wanted to assimilate into the mainstream. When these younger alumni talked about their hopes and aspirations, they were couched in terms of incremental improvements, not radical transformations.

The liberal-arts college was remembered with great fondness by younger Baby Boomers. But unlike their older counterparts, as this group moved through the various stages of their lives, they deliberately shed the past because of too many pressing demands competing for their attention in the present.

It's a Small, Small World

Younger alumni were most focused on what directly impacted the lives of their family, friends, colleagues, and neighbors. They were very derisive of older Baby Boomers, whom they saw as being completely obsessed with their careers or "the world at large," usually to the exclusion of what was right in front of them. Graduates of the 1980s didn't consider a successful career their ultimate goal; it was a means to an end. They were extremely devoted parents and wanted to play an active role in their children's lives.

Rather than re-engaging with their past, they invested emotionally and financially in their children's future. If the choice was between the schools their children currently attended, versus the college they themselves had attended in the past, there was no choice. Supporting their college alma mater evoked a sense of nostalgia, but supporting their children's school was a gift from the heart; it was all about love.

"Helping those in their own community was appealing, because it afforded the opportunity to observe, first hand, the tangible results of their generosity."

Emotional-trigger research revealed the extent to which this group cared deeply about the "here and now." They were most passionate when recounting stories that reinforced their sense of community. They supported people who touched their daily lives. Younger Baby Boomers needed to know their contributions made a difference. Above all, they wanted to know they had impacted someone else's life for the better. Helping those in their own community was appealing, because it afforded the opportunity to observe, firsthand, the tangible results of their generosity. Repeatedly they talked about their charitable contributions in a results-oriented context. It wasn't enough to hope their money made a difference; they demanded the satisfaction of actually witnessing it put to good use. They preferred local efforts, because they knew they were improving the overall quality of life for those within their own community who needed it most.

Pushing the Wrong Buttons

Typically when seeking donations for major fundraising campaigns, the college focused on capital expenditures, endowments, and general operating budgets. That was the problem. They were "abstract" causes that held little appeal. Younger Baby Boomers were moved by personal experiences and personal observations. Most viewed themselves as humanitarians dedicated to helping lift people up. It was easy to overlook a request for money to fund something intangible. So that's exactly what they did: they easily overlooked the request.

Again and again, the younger Baby Boomers expressed an interest in people, rather than in financial causes that were rejected as being too vague. As they saw it, there was an obvious distinction. Financial causes were fungible. The dollars were moved around on the basis of expediency. They had no idea what became of their money. More importantly, they had no idea if anyone actually benefited as a result of their contribution. On the other hand, they had very clear ideas about what helping people meant. To their way of thinking, it meant providing scholarships, improving faculty salaries to attract and retain a high caliber of instructors, and reducing class sizes to improve the overall academic experience. In particular, they would be most inclined to make a donation if a compelling personal appeal was built around scholarship.

Many who saw themselves as humanitarians had not made contributions in the past, because the college failed to engage them emotionally. They repeatedly criticized the school for appeals that were too generic. Emotional-trigger research provided a key insight into what would motivate younger Baby Boomers to make a generous gift. They felt an obligation to give back; the possibility of helping recreate for another student an experience that had been so meaningful in their own life was a powerful draw. Alumni who had received financial aid themselves were especially receptive to passing along the same opportunity to another needy student. This group wanted to feel noble. They wanted to feel good about themselves. And they wanted to know, really know, that their contribution had changed someone's life.

If We Throw a Party, Will They Come?

The college was right about the younger Baby Boomers' interest in people; they just concentrated on the wrong people! Most of these younger graduates had neither the time nor the interest to attend reunions. Similarly, local alumni events and social functions held no allure. Although reconnecting with college friends would certainly be pleasant, it was far down on their list of priorities. No, they weren't about to board that bus for a trip down Memory Lane. What happened in the past stayed in the past, and that's how they wanted it.

These "upstarts" were really throwing the development officers for a loop. Alumni in their 50s and 60s had always enjoyed interaction with their peers. They liked attending social functions and other special events. They understood the game and had the decency to play by the rules. But these younger Baby Boomers weren't even trying! In the same way they rebuffed the "abstract" for the "personal," they shunned opportunities to reconnect with their past in favor of concentrating on their present.

The reason younger graduates failed to respond to reunions, parties, or other alumni activities is because they dismissed the notion that everything should be about them. If they cared about

> **"The right message was being delivered to the absolutely wrong audience."**

anyone, if anyone deserved their time and attention, it was the students. After all, wasn't that the point? Development officers had mistakenly operated on the assumption that the same tactics that worked with older Baby Boomers would be equally effective with graduates from the 1980s. It was a flawed assumption. Not only did younger graduates reject the emphasis on career, in favor of family and community, they were equally vehement about rejecting what they saw as the self-absorption of older Baby Boomers. They criticized 1970s graduates for caring as much about the personal recognition they received as they did about the causes they supported. Unlike many of their predecessors, younger Boomers didn't crave the same kind of attention. Making a small, but real, difference in someone's life was enough. They didn't want to attend social gatherings simply to acknowledge or congratulate one another. The right message was being delivered to the absolutely wrong audience.

Students were the people who mattered; they were the ones who ignited the fire in younger alumni. Once the catchall of "students" morphed into the reality of just one "student," things started to get interesting. That's when younger graduates began to imagine how they could personally make a difference. Their creative juices started flowing.

When younger Baby Boomers thought back to their own college years, they were overwhelmingly positive, except when it came to career counseling and job placement. They had felt unprepared to tackle the world at large. They didn't know how to package their liberal-arts degree or market themselves to potential employers. Even worse, they had no idea what types of jobs were available, what those jobs entailed, or how to find them. But no one realized that this perceived weakness might be the very hook to reel in younger Baby Boomers.

Emotional-trigger research exposed the degree to which the values, needs, and beliefs of younger Baby Boomers differed from their elders. It pointed up the contrasts and the need for this liberal-arts college to rethink their fundraising strategies.

Emotional Trigger	What Emotional Triggers Revealed
Values	▫ They valued an individual over an abstract cause. ▫ They valued the "here and now."
Needs	▫ They needed to know their money had made a difference in someone's life. ▫ They needed to witness the concrete results of their charitable donations.

| Beliefs | ⊡ They believed students, not alumni functions, should be the focus of their time and attention. |
| | ⊡ They believed that improving the students' academic experience was far more important than capital expenditures. |

Personalizing the Appeal

Younger Baby Boomers, as the emotional-trigger research made clear, had a need to be needed. They had a strong penchant for adopting manageable projects that offered demonstrable results. They also prized the academic experience over capital expenditures, operating budgets, or other "lofty" initiatives. Combining these two values presented the college with an opportunity to increase contributions for scholarship by personalizing the appeal and repositioning it from a commendable cause to a presentation of "worthy flesh and blood students" in need of help.

Rather than simply making a donation to a "fund," younger alumni learned how they would make a difference in the lives of individual students. The message, delivered in person, on CD or DVD, by phone, via e-mail or letters, in a brochure, or as a wrap around the Alumni Bulletin, repeatedly spoke to how their gift helped lift people up, one student at a time.

Through a series of stories, the college introduced individual students to this new donor pool. It shared information about who they were, what they'd accomplished, areas of academic interest, extracurricular activities, and, above all, their hopes and dreams for the future. Whether in print, on CDs or DVDs sent to younger alumni, or through some other delivery method, suddenly potential scholarship recipients were no longer strangers. Younger Baby Boomers may have been able to refuse a donation for a line item within a budget, but they couldn't turn away from real students with real and pressing needs.

How Can I Help You? Let Me Count the Ways

The college's perceived weakness with career counseling and job placement provided another meaningful way to re-engage younger Baby Boomers. Many of these potential first-time donors were now senior executives within their companies, successful professionals, or wealthy entrepreneurs. Across the board, they believed there was more than one way they could make a contribution. Most considered their time as valuable as their money. Developing a program to recruit them as mentors proved particularly enticing.

It afforded them the ability to make a tangible difference on a manageable scale in the life of one student. Once they came to know and care about that student, they inevitably became more involved. Because of their commitment to be a mentor, the college was no longer part of their distant past. Now, it was a very real and important part of the "here and now."

Structuring a mentoring relationship offered considerable flexibility. Sessions could be scheduled over breaks or during summer vacation, at which time students would gain familiarity with what a particular career entailed, the skill sets required, what post graduate work might be necessary, how best to design their resume, and how to tackle the job search. Alumni were asked to add their names to a potential summer intern pool that matched them with interested students. Ongoing coaching programs enabled students to receive guidance an hour a week, by phone, during the school year, and more aggressive efforts were made to encourage alumni to recruit at the college.

In a reversal of traditional roles, it was the liberal-arts college that learned an important lesson. Emotional-trigger research demonstrated how humanizing the pitch by telling stories about individual students and creating substantive ways to help them one-on-one coaxed young Baby Boomers to open their wallets. And that's exactly what happened.

SUMMING UP
MARKETING TO DONORS

Situation

A well respected liberal-arts college, preparing to launch a multi-year fundraising campaign, sought to double the amount of contributions they had raised several years earlier. Historically, they had relied on a small group of patrons to subsidize the school, but such a practice left the institution vulnerable should even a few anticipated pledges fail to materialize. The success of future endeavors required cultivating a more comprehensive pipeline of second-tier donors. Efforts to create such a pipeline routinely included reunions, local alumni association functions, letters from the college president, e-mail solicitations, school updates, and an alumni magazine. But such initiatives did little to engage graduates from the 1980s, many of whom were now in a position to afford their first significant gift. These graduates were an absolute enigma to college officials and the board of trustees. So, in anticipation of the upcoming fundraising campaign, emotional-trigger research was conducted to understand how best to engage these individuals.

Alumni Emotional Triggers

The 1980s alumni rejected the "change the world" mantra of older Baby Boomers who came of age during the turbulent 1960s. Rather than changing the world, they wanted to assimilate into the mainstream. They cared deeply about what impacted the daily life of their family, friends, and community. Conversely, they were distrustful of abstract causes. Rather than lifting up humanity, they wanted the immediate and concrete satisfaction associated with lifting up an individual.

Genuine Insight

Although the college was remembered with great fondness, 1980s graduates shed the past in favor of the present. Alumni functions and general solicitations held no allure. They cared about people, not capital expenditures or social gatherings. They wanted to know they'd made a tangible difference in someone's life.

Solution

By focusing on personalized humanitarian appeals, rather than solicitations for general campaign funds or social gatherings, 1980s alumni became more engaged. They responded to stories about worthy students, and they embraced opportunities to serve as mentors. Shifting the focus from a request for money to an opportunity to change a student's life made all the difference. Once they became emotionally invested, the money followed.

Chapter 12

Repositioning a Business

The Emotional Triggers That Rescued a Newly Integrated Company

At times, there's an advantage to being first and staking your claim. Just as often, there's a benefit to letting another company do the heavy lifting, so you can evaluate the situation and zero in on untapped opportunities.

> The greatest problem in communication is the illusion that it has been accomplished.
> —George Bernard Shaw

This is such a story. A particular sector of the global offshore industry had been dominated by one supplier that operated as a virtual monopoly. Customers, eager to regain leverage over pricing and support services, encouraged an infusion of competition into the marketplace. In response to this demand, another international offshore conglomerate, known for their specialty niche businesses, prepared to compete with the fierce market leader by acquiring and merging smaller companies into one vertically integrated operation. Emotional-trigger research revealed how this company, though seemingly positioned to thrive, had inadvertently sabotaged their own success. Once they understood the emotional reasons that kept prospective customers away, they took corrective steps that quickly expanded their market share.

171

LESSON #9

> Control your message before your competition does it for you.

The Absence of Choice

For decades, this segment of the offshore global market had only one major supplier capable of meeting their end-to-end needs. This supplier offered a highly respected product and was praised for their field-support team. But as the only game in town, the amount of influence they exerted over the marketplace rankled customers. And when product demand outstripped their capacity to fill orders, customers were forced to accept delays that put their own businesses at risk. The balance of power had shifted entirely to the supplier, and customers didn't like it. As they frequently asserted, they controlled the purse strings so why shouldn't they call the shots? In the absence of choice, they lost their leverage.

At Long Last

A second global offshore company, sensing customer demand for choice, prepared to capitalize on this unmet need. Initially hampered by fragmented relationships with many of their larger customers, they began by establishing a vertically integrated company capable of competing on the world stage. To satisfy the needs of customers who wanted single sourcing for a comprehensive range of products and services, they purchased two smaller companies to augment their existing product line. Merging the two new acquisitions with their own business enabled them to create end-to-end sales offerings that rivaled those of the industry leader. As they envisioned it, their new, vertically-integrated operation provided customers with a twofold benefit: one-stop shopping, and an alternative to the sole global competitor that dominated the marketplace.

Why Worry? Be Happy!

There are never any guarantees in business, but sometimes it's possible to get pretty close. Or at least it appears that way. Every-

> **"Everyone involved in this venture was confident it had all the earmarks of a sure thing."**

one involved in this venture was confident it had all the earmarks of a sure thing. Each of the three smaller companies, which were now integrated into one end-to-end operation, had been highly regarded in their own right. Each was credited with manufacturing dependable, top-of-the-line products, and each had a reputation for innovation within their respective niche.

So when this "sure thing" was met with a surprisingly lukewarm reception, management was ill-equipped to respond. They had invested in two major acquisitions and reorganized their entire organization to provide customers with the very choice they had repeatedly sought. Rather than enthusiastically rewarding them with new business, however, customers greeted the company's expanded offering with widespread hesitancy and doubt.

This was a highly unusual and baffling case. When choice was finally introduced into the marketplace, it produced anxiety in the very customers who had wanted it for years. Taken aback by this unexpected response, management needed insights into the hidden reasons behind customer resistance. Emotional-trigger research was commissioned to uncover those reasons and use the insights as the basis for solving the problem.

Feelings, Nothing More Than Feelings

Customers often talk tough. Frequently, they will justify demands or rationalize actions by invoking logic. But as we've discussed throughout this book, logic is objective and impersonal. Logic fails to expose the emotions that really drive sales. What customers say and what they actually feel can be very different. When talk collides with feelings, feelings trump talk every time.

It was a lesson the new, vertically integrated company learned the hard way.

Global offshore customers had come to rely on the market leader to meet their end-to-end needs. Such an arrangement simplified the ease of doing business. It streamlined paperwork, cut down on endless sourcing, guaranteed quality products, ensured a high level of service support, and lent a degree of predictability to the entire transaction.

Regardless of these advantages, emotional-trigger research revealed there was an aspect to this arrangement that made customers uneasy, if not defensive. While deep down they may actually have been comfortable with the relationship, they wanted to avoid the appearance of having ceded too much authority to a vendor. It had little to do with how they felt and everything to do with how they wanted to be perceived. So when customers met with smaller specialty companies, they voiced a desire for choice, complained of extended delivery times they had to endure, and bemoaned the lack of a healthy, competitive environment. On an intellectual level, what customers said made sense. More importantly, it satisfied a need to position themselves as objective authorities. Suppliers seeking to do more business with global offshore companies took them at their word. They genuinely believed customers wanted and would support a more competitive marketplace. Customers apparently believed the same thing, until they were confronted with the real possibility of change.

Prospective customers were suddenly unwilling to back up their words with concrete actions. Instead of embracing the new, vertically integrated company as a positive development, they were apprehensive. The theoretical had become real. Now the responsibility of making the wrong decision rested solely on their shoulders. The flip side of the reasons customers initially gave for wanting choice were now the very reasons that unnerved them.

As customers became more engaged in the conversations, it became obvious that their reasons for previously advocating increased competition came from their heads. When speaking with smaller suppliers, they framed the conversation in ways that were politically correct. Senior executives who controlled multi-million dollar contracts didn't want to be seen as complicit in an overly cozy relationship with a major supplier, so they advocated the need for marketplace competition. They claimed to welcome the increased pricing elasticity and service concessions that such competition would inevitably bring. They said all the right things. They gave all the right objective, impersonal answers. But they never talked about what they felt. They never revealed the emotional trigger that was the potential undoing of the new company.

It was true that customers disliked being dependent on a sole supplier, who at times was unable to satisfy all their product needs. On the other hand, the market leader was proving to be a fierce competitor they were afraid of alienating. The power had resided with this

"While having options looked good on paper, there was little internal fortitude for the potential negative consequences of stirring the pot."

market leader for so long, customers no longer questioned the arrangement. Would upending the relationship, seizing control, and expanding the number of key vendors with whom they did business subject them to punitive measures? It seemed like a real possibility. The market leader embarked on a campaign to play on their fears. Although having options looked good on paper, there was little internal fortitude for the potential negative consequences of stirring the pot.

Be Careful What You Wish For

Once customers finally had a legitimate end-to-end supply alternative, they were left to wrestle with conflicting emotional triggers. Balancing the pros and cons of remaining with the market leader, versus giving business to a competing vendor, left them feeling trapped in a proverbial "damned if we do, damned if we don't" scenario. They were unprepared for the rush of emotion that unexpectedly colored their deliberations. Up to the point when the marketplace dynamic actually shifted, customers sincerely believed that they wanted a viable choice. Now they weren't so sure. To the new company's chagrin, prospective customers didn't seem pleased that their wish for increased competition had been granted.

An Emotional Impasse

Emotions regarding the new offshore company were mixed. Separately, each of the three acquisitions that now comprised the new organization had been acclaimed for superior technology and product innovation. But would the merger of these three independent companies be a boon for customers? They needed reassurance and specifics regarding how these assets would be leveraged for their benefit.

Prospective customers were anxious. How would additional competition impact them directly? Would the three niche companies, now part of the vertically integrated organization, coalesce into one seamless operation? Would they simply become another behemoth, subjecting them to all the bureaucratic problems that came with size? Could they trust this new supplier to honor delivery and service commitments? Would the company be distracted by internal merger and acquisition issues? They worried when the market leader insinuated that the new company would focus on containing costs rather than satisfying customer needs. Fearing the new organization's internal priorities would take precedence over their needs, customers were particularly susceptible to efforts by their long-time supplier to exploit their fears of slow response times, sporadic service, and increased red tape. The market leader's skillful attempts to manipulate and distort reality were working. Prospective customers were duly intimidated.

Provoked by the market leader, customers bought into the suggestion that the new organization's strategy was to increase prices. They grew concerned that arrogance would overcome common sense and lead to price gouging. When customers were led to believe the real aim of the merger was expense control, not the introduction of an alternative end-to-end source of supply, they were easily convinced. When they were warned that each of the smaller companies had inadequate staffing levels to meet their regional needs, they panicked. So, rather than viewing the merger in a favorable light, the market leader had artfully exploited customer insecurities, potential liabilities, and unsubstantiated assertions to discourage client defections.

The truth was very different than the picture painted by their competition, but the newly integrated company had left prospective customers frustrated and uninformed. When asked for specific materials, none were available. The new, vertically integrated operation had put bodies on the street to introduce the new company, but failed to equip them with the tools they needed to communicate their story. The only materials they had contained a global message, rather than a localized one for each international location. It was the antithesis of what prospective customers valued and did not bode well for the future.

Emotional-trigger research revealed that prospective customers' rational desire for competitive choice was overpowered by their emotional fear of the consequences. Their resistance to the new supplier was swayed by seeds of doubt, planted and nurtured by the market leader.

EMOTIONAL TRIGGER	WHAT EMOTIONAL TRIGGERS REVEALED
Feelings	▣ They were anxious the new supplier would focus on internal merger considerations at the expense of customer needs.
	▣ They were worried the new competitor would emphasize cost cutting measures, resulting in reduced service levels.

	▫ They were apprehensive the new company would not be sensitive to local concerns, their number one priority. ▫ They were fearful the lack of information about the new company had sinister meaning. ▫ They were afraid of jeopardizing their relationship with the market leader.
Needs	▫ They needed assurances the new company would leverage the technology expertise and product innovation of the three smaller companies for their benefit. ▫ They needed to have a comfort level that the new company would be able to honor delivery commitments on time and on budget. ▫ They needed guarantees that the new company would be adequately staffed to handle regional demands.

Letting the Competition Define You Is Never a Good Thing

The new company had allowed a dangerous communications vacuum to develop in the marketplace. They had been so preoccupied with the logistics of establishing their end-to-end sales offering, they failed to control their own message. They neglected to develop a comprehensive strategy for positioning their new company with prospective customers. Instead they assumed the benefits were obvious and that customers would automatically reward them for providing an end-to-end alternative. Well, the market leader had no intention of letting that happen!

With no comprehensive message coming from the new company, the market leader pounced to fill the void. They seized control of the "story" and told it to their advantage. The new company had been defined by their competition. Now they were in the unenviable position of playing defense. Misinformation had been widely disseminated and had to be countered. Unfortunately, the misinformation had accomplished its goal and fueled the fears of prospective customers. It was one thing to correct facts. It was quite another to quell emotional reactions.

> **"The new company had been defined by their competition. Now they were in the unenviable position of playing defense."**

Customers needed to hear directly from the company about how the new organization would positively affect their professional lives, and quickly, to blunt the damage caused by the market leader. Until that happened, customers would emotionally resist switching business from a long-time supplier to the new market entrant.

Control the Message

Management reassessed the local sales territories to determine if staffing coverage was adequate and to reaffirm that the existing staff had both the skills and training to do their jobs effectively. As necessary, staff was added, trained, or replaced to ensure customers received the caliber of service that had emerged as one of their core emotional triggers. In contrast to the impressions conveyed by the market leader, customers experienced a vendor who listened to their concerns and responded to their emotional need for strong, local service support. The result had a calming effect and gave the new company time to formulate their message.

Once immediate steps had been taken to reassure customers, the company's top priority was to create very targeted and informative messages. A communications plan was developed to explain why this new entity had been created. Every aspect of the message was presented as a response to the emotional-trigger research. Whether it was how the new company would tangibly improve customers' business lives, the value the company brought to the marketplace overall, or how they differed from the existing market leader, everything was positioned in the context of customers' specific emotional needs.

Collateral sales materials, in combination with a trade advertising campaign, reinforced the message, established the brand promise, and armed sales people with a cohesive package explaining the company's market positioning. But the communications plan went beyond just a message. It included a strategy for instilling confidence in prospective customers and forging relationships with them. Senior management held one-on-ones meetings with every customer group to personally answer their questions and solicit input on how to become their vendor of choice. The company president called key customers to discuss their issues and schedule time for personal visits. Every step along the way, customers were kept in the loop. Every new service initiative, product offering, or technology innovation was communicated through comprehensive sales materials, in-person meetings, timely phone updates, field trips, and the Internet.

From the beginning, the new company's problems had more to do with perception than reality. Their products were high quality. Their support team was dedicated and service oriented. Their technology expertise was the best in the industry, and they were renowned for product design innovation. These advantages, combined with competitive pricing and unparalleled delivery turnaround times, made them an attractive end-to-end supplier for their industry segment. Repositioning their business against a formidable market leader elicited strong emotional reactions that almost proved their undoing, because they neglected to take ownership of their message. Once armed with the insights uncovered during emotional-trigger research, they found ways to dispel rumors, differentiate their company from the industry leader, and speak to the emotional concerns that won over large numbers of prospective new customers.

SUMMING UP
REPOSITIONING A BUSINESS

Situation

A company in the global offshore industry acquired two smaller companies in order to augment their existing product line and create an "end-to-end" sales opportunity. As they envisioned it, their new, vertically integrated operation offered customers a twofold benefit: one-stop shopping, and an alternative to the sole global competitor that dominated the marketplace. For years this formidable competitor had been the only game in town. Customers, eager to regain leverage over pricing and support services, encouraged the infusion of competitive alternatives. But when the new company, in response to specific demand, entered the market with quality products, strong field support, and an international reputation for innovation, customers stayed away. Emotional-trigger research was used to expose the reasons for customer resistance.

The Customers' Emotional Triggers

Prospective customers were anxious. Provoked by the market leader, they bought into assertions that the new company had vertically integrated their business only to engage in price gouging and cost containment measures at the expense of field support services. They were frightened if they took business away from their long-term supplier, they'd be subjected to punitive consequences. They worried the new organization's issues would take priority over their own needs. And, in the absence of any specifics, they were afraid to risk the known—no matter how imperfect—for the unknown.

Genuine Insight

The company had allowed a dangerous communications vacuum to develop in the marketplace. They had been so preoccupied with logistics, they had failed to take control of their message. Instead, their major competitor jumped in to fill the void and negatively framed their story.

Solution

First management reassessed local sales territories to ensure adequate staffing levels and reaffirm the technical expertise of those individuals. As necessary, they trained, added, or replaced members of the support teams. Once accomplished, it had a calming effect on prospective customers. Then the company's top priority turned to creating very targeted and informative messages explaining why the new entity was developed and how customers would benefit. Every aspect of the message from collateral materials, to trade advertising to senior management meetings with customer groups, to personal calls from or meetings with the company president was positioned as a specific response to customers' emotional needs, revealed through the emotional-trigger research. Once armed with the reasons customers had stayed away, the new market entrant responded quickly. They found ways to dispel rumors, differentiate their company from the industry leader, and successfully increase their market share.

Part IV

Putting Emotional Triggers to Work—Customer Relationships

Chapter 13

Benchmarking Customer Satisfaction

The Emotional Triggers That Saved 20 Million Dollars

Now and then, everyone finds themselves between a rock and a hard place. Although it's never comfortable to be in that situation, at least most of us recognize when it's happening. We personally know one senior

> The most important thing in communication is to hear what isn't being said.
> —Peter F. Drucker

executive who didn't. This is the story about a successful marketing agency with smart leadership that almost lost a 20-million dollar account they didn't even realize was at risk. At a crucial juncture, emotional-trigger research exposed critical insights top management needed to save the contract and continue the association.

LESSON #10

Personal dynamics do not equal a solid business relationship.

Edward's Story

The executive, let's call him "Edward," headed the largest office of a leading international agency known for specialty marketing and, ironically, customer relationship management. His branch represented more than two-thirds of the division's entire income. The agency, in turn, was part of a highly regarded holding company with an extensive portfolio of global communications businesses in a number of interrelated disciplines.

This agency was thriving. Revenue had grown by double digits for almost a decade. Their biggest accounts billed more each year, and new accounts were continually added to the roster. Although the picture was rosy, top management understood this rate of growth wasn't sustainable. There was a limit to how much additional revenue current accounts would generate, and, if for no other reason than potential conflicts of interest, the rate of customer acquisition would inevitably slow down as well. They were in the process of transitioning from an early-stage growth business to one confronting the challenges of a larger and more mature operation. It was a transition that required great care, because they had to meet the demands of larger, long-term accounts, while simultaneously satisfying expectations of their more recent clients. Success depended upon a combination of insight and finesse.

Edward wanted impartial, third-party assessments of client satisfaction among all levels of management at their largest Fortune 500 accounts. He wanted to know how clients evaluated his agency's job performance. Were their needs and expectations being met? How did they characterize the agency's quality of work, client support, and, strategic expertise? What, if anything, was changing inside his clients' organizations and how might those changes affect the relationship dynamics? The plan was to conduct emotional-trigger research interviews with senior and middle management executives at each of the targeted companies.

Perception Versus Reality

For eight years, Edward boarded a plane once a month and flew several hours, so he could personally meet with the agency's largest client. He routinely participated in many of their planning, creative, and strategy sessions. During his visits he met with both top management and others throughout the marketing division. He believed the association to be especially strong at every level. Given his assumption, he suggested this company serve as the benchmark, against which all other agency accounts would be judged. But from the start, these interviews revealed a serious disconnect between Edward's perception and the client reality. Even as the interviews were taking place, the client was undergoing a new agency review. If this was the benchmark against which all other relationships were to be judged, Edward was in real trouble.

Everyone at the account admitted Edward had no idea a review was underway. Senior executives, as well as more junior staff, all described Edward in glowing terms. They said he was extremely smart. Both his creative and strategic skills were praised. He was considered a genuinely nice and sincere person whose integrity was beyond reproach. And, to top it off, he was liked by one and all. Something didn't add up. When this was pointed out during the interviews, the respondents looked away. They fidgeted, they squirmed, and they extracted promises that whatever they said would not be attributed back to them.

We Got to Have It: Just a Little Respect

Slowly the truth trickled out. Yes, Edward was nice. He was more than nice. He was really nice. That was the problem. It's one thing to be accommodating to your client, but they faulted him for being too nice when it came to running his own operation. They felt he repeatedly acquiesced to his staff. He empowered them to the detriment of agency accounts.

When the creative team met with the client, they were given specific objectives and directions. Too often, they ignored the client's

wishes. Approval was never sought before embarking on a different approach; they just went their own way. In the process, they
invariably submitted work that was not on message, went over
budget, and missed important deadlines. To make matters worse,
Edward let them get away with it; he didn't rein in the creative
staff because he didn't want to demoralize them. He was so big on
"empowerment," that in his effort not to rock the boat, he almost
sank the ship! The client felt they were the victims of excessive
accommodation to agency egos. All and all, it was infuriating, and
they'd had enough.

When associates at the company started to discuss why they
were undertaking a new agency search, they offered rational and
objective reasons. The creative recommendations failed to reflect
their priorities. The agency often disregarded the parameters they
were given. Frequently work was over-budget or submitted late.
By any measure, these were perfectly logical and acceptable reasons to look elsewhere. Everything they said was accurate, but it
wasn't real. There was more to the story. Reasons are one thing,
emotional triggers are quite another.

What was the emo-
tional trigger? What fi-
nally put a 20-million
dollar account at risk? The
"What finally put a 20-million dollar account at risk?"
client resented feeling "dismissed." It was insulting, an arrogant
display of disrespect. They said egos were running amok. And,
most galling of all, it seemed to be okay. What the client said
didn't seem to matter. Who was working for whom?

Edward Kept in the Dark

This apparent lack of regard hit a raw nerve and triggered a
decision to look for another agency, but a piece of the puzzle was
still missing. The client may have been angry with the creative
staff, but they were glowing when it came to Edward. So how was
it possible the relationship had deteriorated so badly, and he

remained clueless? Inevitably, during each of the interviews, the obvious question was asked. Had they shared their concerns with Edward? They had not. No one wanted to broach the subject; senior executives were the most uncomfortable. The executive vice president was especially ill at ease. After skirting the issue he finally blurted out, "How do you tell someone you like, who you've worked with for eight years, that you don't approve of the way he manages his business?" He preferred to hide behind more palatable reasons, rather than risk offending Edward.

He wasn't alone. No one wanted to criticize Edward, at least not to his face. They worried about hurting his feelings. From their perspective, criticism of his management style was tantamount to expressing a lack of confidence in him, but that's exactly what they ended up doing. By deciding to look for another agency, they tacitly assumed Edward was incapable of fixing the problem. Without the emotional-trigger research, he would never have had the chance to salvage the business, because he wouldn't have known it was in jeopardy.

Conflicting Emotional Triggers

The widespread resentment at feeling dismissed existed at all levels within the client's organization. Then there was the misguided sense of loyalty to Edward that placed his "feelings" above his "interests." Finally, the idea of directly criticizing him made the client very uneasy; they wanted to avoid such an exchange at all costs. Outrage at the creative team, combined with genuine affection for Edward and a desire to preserve that amicable relationship, was a dangerous combination of conflicting emotions.

No one suggested Edward would be defensive or indifferent. The hesitancy to confront him really wasn't about Edward. It was about how they'd feel having to criticize and potentially hurt him. No one wanted to be the one to do it.

Much later, after they'd replaced his agency, he'd be given an explanation that wasn't too disagreeable, but he would never have known the truth. He'd have the facts but he'd still lack genuine insight. Perhaps the incident would have prodded him to tinker around the edges of the real problem, only for it to surface again later with another client. And he still would never know why.

The Danger of "Inside Out" Thinking

It's unlikely the creative team was unaware of the resentment their behavior provoked. It was equally unlikely they were going to share this information with Edward. Critical insights he needed to manage the business were in conflict with their own self interest. Who would voluntarily announce to their boss a major account was routinely displeased with them? No one without a sizeable trust fund! Instead, they depicted the client as unreasonable, demanding, and devoid of strategic vision. The creative team wasn't the problem. The problem was a difficult client. No matter how hard they tried, nothing pleased them.

Edward made the same mistake that afflicts many organizations. He got sucked into the trap of "inside out" thinking. He was surrounded by employees who reinforced a singular point of view, so he chose to believe what he heard. He was overly supportive. His passivity, combined with a willingness to accept an insular and skewed perspective, nearly cost him the agency's largest account.

Let's examine the crucial emotional triggers that provoked a new agency search.

EMOTIONAL TRIGGER	WHAT EMOTIONAL TRIGGERS REVEALED
Patterns of Behavior	⊡ The client was continually subjected to a dysfunctional work relationship that cost them extra money, caused them to miss deadlines, and involved constant power struggles with the creative team. ⊡ The narratives painted an upside-down picture in which the creative team behaved as if they were calling the shots.
Passions	⊡ The client was outraged that the creative team ignored their input and felt no obligation to discuss it.
Feelings	⊡ The client felt dismissed. ⊡ The client felt very uncomfortable at the thought of criticizing Edward directly about his management style.
Needs	⊡ The client needed to preserve their notion of "friendship" with Edward by avoiding a confrontation that might hurt his feelings.

Success!

Fortunately, emotional-trigger research provided Edward with crucial input he wouldn't have otherwise received. The client wasn't going to tell him. Members of the account management team, who had more than a passing inkling into the problem, were also reluctant to tell him. They didn't want to point fingers at the creative department. And clearly the creative team was keeping quiet.

Once he learned the truth about the underlying emotional triggers that drove the decision to replace his agency, Edward took action. Armed with very specific insight, he turned the situation around. First he re-engineered the strategic and creative planning process. Specific metrics relative to deadlines, costs, timetables, and client input at various stages of the job were put in place. Both the account management and creative teams were held accountable for compliance. It was a non-negotiable issue.

Edward became more directly involved. Instead of acting as a benevolent patron, he became the manager. He participated in regularly scheduled meetings at key intervals to ensure work met the agency's creative and strategic standards. He was adamant it be on time, on specification, and on budget. "No surprises" became the new mantra. If potential problems were identified in advance, he worked with his team to solve them. But if commitments weren't honored and he was caught unaware, the offender would be terminated. This sense of discipline affected every aspect of how the agency interacted with clients. It also demanded improved coordination and planning within and between all internal departments. Finally, he spearheaded an agency-wide "attitude readjustment," by emphasizing what was expected of employees in a service business.

The client was impressed with the openness and speed with which Edward tackled the problem. After several months, the client, appreciative that their concerns had been taken seriously, was thrilled with the agency's newfound responsiveness. The search for a new agency was suspended. Instead, Edward's agency was rewarded with a two-year renewal contract.

Summing Up

Benchmarking Customer Satisfaction

Situation

A leading international specialty marketing agency was transitioning from an early stage growth business to a larger and more mature operation. Edward, the head of the largest branch office, wanted to assess client satisfaction and commissioned an independent third party to conduct emotional-trigger research. For eight years, he visited monthly with his largest Fortune 500 account and believed this relationship to be particularly strong. Despite their frequency, the interviews revealed the client had actually initiated a new agency search without first notifying Edward. Although they were extremely positive about him personally, they felt the creative team was out of control. Instead of following directions, they dismissed the client's requests when they disagreed and, without ever discussing it, took a different approach. The problem was seen as Edward's management style; he empowered his team to the client's detriment. Although the creative team was aware of the problem, they didn't intend to enlighten Edward. Meanwhile, the client, in a misguided attempt to spare Edward's feelings, made things worse. They preferred to switch agencies, rather than offend him or engage in an unpleasant confrontation.

The Client's Emotional Triggers

The client felt outrage at being dismissed by the creative team, yet they felt a personal need to preserve their friendship with Edward. They were uncomfortable criticizing his management style or engaging in a frank dialogue that might hurt his feelings.

Genuine Insight

"Operational problems" was the comfortable answer for undergoing a new agency search. It was factual, but it wasn't the hidden reason. What really tipped the scales was that the client felt dismissed by the agency's creative team. Rather than being treated with respect, they were put on the defensive, and they intensely resented that feeling.

Solution

For the first time, Edward came to recognize how he had inadvertently put his agency at risk. Instead of operating as the senior manager, he had assumed the role of a benevolent patron. The solution was a complete re-engineering of the agency's strategic and creative planning process. Edward instituted new internal performance metrics that were strictly enforced. He put the "service" back into his service business. As a result, rather than losing the account, they signed a two year renewal agreement worth 20 million dollars.

Chapter 14

Turning Around a Company in Crisis

The Emotional Triggers That Stemmed Co-Op Member Defections

Companies in crisis often point to one significant occurrence as the cause of their troubles. Maybe that's the case; maybe not. But one thing is certain: a turnaround effort must be based on solving the right problems, or it won't work. Sometimes companies on the brink, in their haste to make things better, grasp at easy answers. But when a single occurrence becomes synonymous with the actual crisis, it can obscure other considerations. This is a story about a struggling cooperative, one of the largest in the United States, that turned to emotional-trigger research as the starting point, instead of as the last resort. By choosing to forgo obvious "facts," and focusing instead on the strong emotions that caused members to desert the organization in large numbers, attrition was drastically reduced and a successful turnaround was well on its way.

> I know you believe what you think I said, but I'm not sure you realize that what you heard is not what I meant.
> —Robert McCloskey

LESSON #11

> Trust is not an expendable commodity.

Shock, Outrage, Desertion

This multi-billion dollar cooperative had thousands of members serving the needs of consumers and commercial enterprises in a combination of four different ventures. For readers who are unfamiliar with cooperatives, they are businesses owned and operated for the benefit of those using its services or buying its products. Members join forces to gain economic power, purchasing strength, goods and services, and marketing opportunities.

Throughout a period of several years, the co-op had grown through a series of mergers. The mergers had not gone smoothly. Different management styles, duplicated staff functions, and internal power struggles added up to one dysfunctional company. But senior executives and the board of directors presented a very different picture to the membership. To hear them tell it, everything was terrific; things couldn't be better. That is, until the day they dropped a bombshell and announced, out of the blue, a surprise loss of more than 100 million dollars. At first the members were stunned. Then they were outraged.

In addition to sales generated by their own businesses, members received dividend checks at the end of each year based on a percentage of the organization's profits. This was money members counted on and factored into their annual operating budgets. Naturally, once the co-op incurred major losses, there were no profits for members to share. Suddenly, without advance warning, all dividend payments stopped. Within the span of a few years the co-op had gone from being highly profitable to one on the verge of financial disaster. Following the announcement of the financial loss and the lack of further dividends, more than 1,500 members had joined competing co-ops and hundreds more were about to leave.

Drastic Circumstances Call for Drastic Measures

The future of the company was extremely precarious. At this point, the major lenders replaced top management and mandated board changes; a new chief executive officer was brought in to stabilize the situation. Reversing the trend of member defections and regaining their trust was pivotal to the co-op's short term survival and subsequent turnaround. They desperately needed to reconnect with the membership, develop meaningful opportunities for growth, and create a persuasive and credible reason to avoid further attrition.

Management Was Positive. Were They Right?

Most senior officers and field executives were positive the explanation for member defections was the co-op's suspension of annual dividend payments. They repeatedly maintained that this single "occurrence" was the reason members were fleeing in droves. The new CEO wanted to test this assumption, in order to understand what really influenced members' decision to leave the co-op and, ultimately, what management had to do to convince them to stay.

Given all the undercurrents rampant within the co-op, conducting emotional-trigger research with high-value members became the first step toward plotting a turnaround strategy. Half of those interviewed were classified as high-risk members and known to be in serious negotiations with competing co-ops. The other half were considered to be typical members who were upset but, up to that point, had refrained from exploring other options. The allegiance among many in this second group, however, was hanging by a thread.

As usual, the truth was more complicated than the facts suggested. No one was happy about losing their dividend payments. Admittedly, it did provoke some disgruntled members to seriously consider joining another co-op, but the majority of members regarded the suspension of dividend payments as symptomatic of something bigger and much more infuriating. The dividend uproar was simply the straw that broke the camel's back, rather than the entire problem like management said it was.

Emotional-trigger research signaled something worse, something that went far beyond the co-op's bottom line. **"Management mistakenly thought the crisis was all about money; it wasn't."** These interviews exposed a widespread hostility toward management that had been hovering just beneath the radar for a long time. When the financial loss was announced, this hostility finally erupted in an avalanche of recriminations and defections. Management mistakenly thought the crisis was all about money; it wasn't. To the membership, it was about integrity and respect. These were the emotional triggers that literally ignited a firestorm from Maine to Hawaii.

The Unforgivable Sin

Individual owners were painfully aware of the problems facing their co-op, but they were shaken more by management's deceit and misrepresentation than by the actual circumstances; that's what they thought was truly unforgivable. After all, it was their co-op. How dare the management team, whom they employed, have the nerve to deliberately mislead them!

Members Weren't Upset; They Were Furious

Many of the members who were straddling the fence about whether to remain with the co-op intended to leave unless there were dramatic changes. Business had to be conducted very differently going forward. That was management's only hope of repairing their frayed relationship with members. Communications had to be open. Commitments had to be honored. More time had to be spent with members around the country. Management had to get out of their "ivory tower" and observe the consequences of their decisions. Above all, members demanded they be treated with integrity and candor. They had no tolerance for posturing. Honesty meant everything. Most would have reacted differently to the financial crisis if management had a track record of owning up to their mistakes and admitting when they were wrong.

Members felt management was arrogant, dismissive, and patronizing. That was clear by the way they'd hidden the truth about the co-op's escalating monetary losses. Not only did members have a right to know what was happening, management had a moral obligation to tell them. They were supposed to serve the membership base, not vice versa. Instead, their refusal to accept responsibility was considered inexcusable. When problems arose, members had difficulty finding anyone to take ownership and help them resolve the situation. Management also consistently failed to deliver on its promises regarding operational issues, financial matters, new programs, or promised system improvements.

Members were offended by how infrequently management made trips to visit with them. When they did show up, many executives breezed in and out as if they always had something better to do. The cultural divide between the corporate group and the membership was enormous. Members wanted to do business with people like them. The importance of the human connection was a strong emotional trigger. They valued individuals who were genuine and down-to-earth, and they expected true partners to roll up their sleeves to help solve problems; instead the management team was aloof. This discrepancy between expectations and reality caused an innate distrust of management aggravating the co-op's woes.

A major sore spot was the endless number of poorly planned and poorly executed programs that management continually introduced. These programs had cost the co-op credibility, goodwill, and revenue, as members who had been previously burned shied away from new initiatives. Too often, the difference between what was promised and what was delivered was unacceptable; members had become jaded. They railed that management didn't appreciate how their decisions negatively affected them, individually, or the co-op overall.

These programs were an emotional trigger, because they represented yet another aspect of management's perceived lack of regard for members. Complaints fell on deaf ears and members were seething. Their opinions were disregarded; worse still, they were rarely solicited. No one seemed overly concerned about the financial or operation limitations of the members. Again and again, management demonstrated their insensitivity. They neglected to streamline and simplify the programs, let alone reduce them.

Most of the problems that arose would have been avoided if management had only listened when members voiced their concerns. It was a radioactive topic. Members fumed that new initiatives **"Members whose concerns were met with a deaf ear were the most likely to sever their association with the co-op. Ignoring their input was offensive."** were never tested in the field. No one did contingency planning. There was inadequate coordination between corporate departments to ensure a smooth execution. And if all that weren't enough, expensive but poorly thought-out programs, made worse by weak sales, resulted in losses that ultimately reduced the co-op's profits.

Members whose concerns were met with a deaf ear were the most likely to sever their association with the co-op. Ignoring their input was offensive. Dismissing outright the value of incorporating their feedback into the advance-planning process was demeaning. When members discussed all these issues they weren't speaking abstractly about their opinions. They were talking about their real need to be treated as equals by management. Their sense of dignity was completely intertwined with their need to be shown respect.

When an Explanation Becomes a Crutch

These needs were pivotal emotional triggers that would ultimately decide the co-op's fate. Management had adopted a blanket explanation regarding why so many members were leaving: the co-op's inability to pay dividends. It had become too convenient of a crutch. In fact, management was using this crutch to deflect attention away from their culpability. Members may have vented their anger and frustration about dividend checks. But their decision to stay or join another co-op often hinged on operational and management issues.

A Beacon of Hope

Members no longer trusted management, but they did trust other members. Because of that trust, a beacon of hope emerged for the co-op. Members considered their peers more credible than corporate executives and turned to them for input or advice. Many members had assumed a leadership role in their respective communities and operated as goodwill ambassadors or mentors. When called upon they always helped.

These larger and more successful members could potentially play a decisive role in turning the co-op around. If this important group of influencers were convinced of management's sincerity and commitment, they would carry considerable sway. They had one huge advantage: other members sincerely believed these individuals had their best interests at heart. If they became advocates for remaining with the co-op, they would accomplish what management could not. Handled correctly, they represented the best opportunity to spread a positive message through word of mouth. But if these leaders questioned management's ability or willingness to make the necessary changes, it would seal the co-op's fate.

Intense emotional triggers emerged during these interviews. The more powerful the trigger, the less it was about money. These triggers were very personal.

EMOTIONAL TRIGGER	WHAT EMOTIONAL TRIGGERS REVEALED
Needs	▫ Members had a need to be treated with respect. ▫ Members had a need to be more than listened to. They wanted to be really heard. ▫ Members had a need to feel valued.
Passions	▫ Members were enraged by what they saw as management's lack of candor and integrity. ▫ Members despised management's attitude and their sense of superiority. ▫ Members resented management's disregard for their operational and financial limitations.
Feelings	▫ Members felt betrayed. ▫ Members felt demeaned when their opinions were ignored, or never even solicited, by management.
Needs	▫ Members valued honesty. ▫ Members valued integrity. ▫ Members valued sincerity. ▫ Members valued people who were direct.

A Cultural Revolution

Because the interviews bared such raw emotional triggers, the solutions required sweeping cultural, operational, and strategic changes. For starters, every element of the turnaround plan had to display a newfound respect for the members and a genuine sensitivity to their sense of betrayal and disenfranchisement. Going forward, their input had to be an integral part of the planning process, and management had to be responsive to that input.

The first order of business was to transform the existing management culture. Survival demanded radically different ways of doing business. The emotional triggers that surfaced during the interviews became the basis for developing a code of conduct. This code encapsulated the operating principles by which the corporate group would be guided in the future. Substance replaced hype. Integrity replaced deception. Active listening replaced patronizing exchanges. Members' priorities replaced those of management. Cross functional planning replaced "ivory tower" dictates.

Given their stature within the co-op, influential members needed to be convinced first. Management had to prove they were focused on the right things, were sincere about making them happen, and had the ability to translate words into action. If this elite group was persuaded, the co-op could enlist their services to help advance the turnaround agenda. They were the best arbiters of potential member reaction in their respective communities. Bringing these individuals in at the preliminary planning stage provided management with valuable feedback, while flattering the members by acknowledging their positions of prominence. Once they were part of the process, they would share ownership of the result, making their support more likely. Finally, their advocacy would enable the co-op to launch a credible grassroots initiative, because it would be the members, not management, spreading a message of real change. Members trusted other members. Influential members, in their dual capacity as leaders and mentors, enjoyed even more authority. Beginning with this select group of members sparked a positive snowball effect. When they chose to remain with the co-op, others did the same.

A Fresh Approach to Planning

Given how toxic the relationship between management and members had become, tackling the cultural issues was the logical starting point. But changes within the culture alone weren't enough to steer the company out of crisis mode. The business had been battered by the loss of more than 100 million dollars. That figure was compounded by the additional loss of revenue associated with the loss of 20 percent of the membership to other co-ops. Sweeping process re-engineering efforts were also necessary. A return to profitability demanded a fresh approach to internal planning. It also demanded management spend more time in the field gaining a "real world" perspective.

Associates at manager level were assigned to work with a member for several days. This helped the corporate team become more familiar with members' businesses and observe, firsthand, the impact of poor decisions made while sequestered in their "ivory tower." The new CEO led the charge. More time was devoted to member interaction and less was spent in corporate meetings limited to headquarters personnel. Member reaction was positive and word-of-mouth began to spread.

Every aspect of the way programs had been conceived, planned, and implemented had to be scrapped. The failure of these programs encapsulated many of the emotional triggers exposed during the emotional-trigger research interviews. Members had a need to be heard. They were passionate about management's refusal to consider their operational and financial limitations. Real world restrictions were never incorporated into the planning process. Making things worse, management didn't share the loss. Members absorbed it all. They felt demeaned when their opinions weren't solicited or when they were patronized. And, having already been burned by the co-op's surprise announcement of a major loss, they valued honesty above all else. Talk was cheap; the programs were not. Management had over promised and under delivered. Members got hype, fanfare, and distortions. What they wanted, and what they felt entitled to, was straight talk.

Management immediately cancelled most of the new programs that had been scheduled to be introduced, and the membership cheered. Then the entire procedure involving future programs was radically overhauled. Cross-functional planning was implemented for all new initiatives. A formalized procedure was put in place to obtain input from all key disciplines for ideas under serious consideration, and, a cross-section of typical members served as the "conscience" of the membership. Previously, management's litmus test for new programs was whether they advanced corporate interests. With members now reviewing every proposal, nothing got out of committee unless everyone stood to benefit.

Selection of the member panels was crucial. Those chosen were individuals who were well known and respected by their peers. Focusing on members who were influencers and leaders was central to every aspect of the co-op's turnaround strategy. This instilled confidence in the process and assured other members they were being heard. Member representation was not a token gesture.

Critical, Sophisticated, and Powerful Insights Lead to Turnaround

During the next two years, cross-functional teams were set up to tackle issues affecting every discipline within the company. Members took notice as the cultural shift and process re-engineering efforts began to coalesce. In large numbers, they elected to remain. The new CEO embraced the emotional triggers unmasked during the interviews and called them critical, sophisticated, and powerful insights that made a significant contribution to the successful turnaround of the co-op. Unquestionably, members were upset about losing their dividend payments. That was a "fact." It just didn't happen to be the hidden reason they had been joining competing co-ops. Emotional-trigger research uncovered the real priorities this company in crisis had to address. Conventional thinking and self-serving assertions would have led them astray. What was "accurate" proved to be something entirely different than what was real.

SUMMING UP
TURNING AROUND A COMPANY IN CRISIS

Situation

Throughout several years, one of the nation's largest co-ops had grown through a series of mergers. The new organization, however, was continually plagued by internal power struggles. During this difficult period, the board of directors had misrepresented the co-op's situation. Members were assured all was going well, right up to the day when an enormous financial loss was announced. At first, members were shocked, and then they were outraged. In addition to being misled, the loss meant the co-op would no longer issue dividend checks. Within just a few years, 20 percent of the membership had joined competing cooperatives, and hundreds more were threatening to leave. Headquarters and field executives were confident the explanation for member attrition was the suspension of dividend payments. But a new CEO, brought in by the lenders, wanted to understand what really influenced a member's decision to leave and what management had to do to convince them to stay. Emotional-trigger research was conducted to answer these questions.

The Memberships' Emotional Triggers

Intensely felt passions and deeply held personal values created a combustible mixture of emotional triggers. The dominant trigger, however, was not about money; it was about relationships. Members felt betrayed. They were enraged by the lack of candor and took offense at what they saw as management's arrogance. As owners they resented being excluded from key decisions that negatively impacted their businesses.

Genuine Insight

Suspension of dividend payments had become the convenient crutch management used to absolve them of culpability. The checks were only a symptom, not the hidden reason. The truth was more human. Members felt disenfranchised by a management team that had no interest in forging real partnerships with their actual employers.

Solution

The corporate culture had to change. A new management code of conduct was implemented. Next, cross functional planning was instituted to ensure future programs benefited both management *and* members. A group of typical members, with an emphasis on individuals who were well known and highly regarded by their peers, comprised part of every project team. These members served as the "conscience" of the co-op. The new corporate culture combined with the operational changes, instilled a newfound confidence among the membership. The attrition rate was drastically reduced, and the turnaround was successfully underway.

Chapter 15

Improving Customer Relationships in a Monopoly Industry

The Emotional Triggers That Interpreted Mixed Messages

Nothing lasts forever. A company that operates as a monopoly today may someday face stiff competition. That's why it's important to establish positive customer relationships before it's too late. This is the story about a utility, operating as a monopoly, that needed commercial/industrial leaders to support pending legislative and regulatory proposals. But before the company could build stronger relationships within this sector, they needed to clarify what appeared to be mixed customer messages. Emotional-trigger research uncovered critical nuances that helped the utility understand the issues that mattered to their customers and respond to them.

> we are drowning in information but starved for knowledge.
> —John Naisbitt

LESSON #12

Even when you don't have to, act like a partner.

They Said What?

This was a company caught in the crosshairs. Under assault from every conceivable angle, management was reeling. The cost of raw materials was soaring. The delivery system was overwhelmed and antiquated. Commercial/industrial customers were livid about spiraling rate increases and beginning to explore alternative options that were emerging. Profit margins—to say nothing of actual profits—were shrinking. Government agencies and the legislature were applying pressure to contain expenses, while simultaneously demanding significant service improvements. Under the best of circumstances, it was a Herculean task.

As if that wasn't enough, a sense of confusion pervaded the organization. Over a number of years, the company had routinely hired industry "experts" to measure satisfaction among commercial customers and, based upon the findings, provide specific actionable recommendations. Mirroring our own personal experience as corporate executives, senior management had shelves overflowing with every imaginable type of report, chart, graph, matrix, ranking, table, diagram, and related statistic. The information was sliced, diced, quantified, and measured on literally scores of dimensions.

They had it all with the singular exception of reliable or insightful answers. Why? Because trying to analyze the data was akin to reading tea leaves. Key "findings" were contradictory, leaving management no closer to understanding how best to connect with their customers. They received high scores for resolving problems quickly, but low scores for being customer-oriented or responding to customer needs. They were praised for delivering a quality service, while simultaneously chastised for decreases in service reliability. They were told it was important to look out for customer safety, even though taking preventative measures were ascribed a low priority. Most significantly, they were warned that commercial/industrial customers were up in arms over rate increases, yet these same reports suggested that customers believed the utility gave them their money's worth.

What on earth did all this mean? No one had a clue. Management was convinced that recent rate increases were at the heart of customer dissatisfaction and bemoaned the fact that, as a regulated industry, it was an issue over which they had little control. Even so, they recognized the company was at a critical juncture. Without the support of their commercial/industrial customer base, any attempt to enlist governmental and regulatory agency cooperation for pending proposals would be non-existent. But before they could hope to forge stronger relationships with these customers, they needed to clarify all the mixed messages. That's when they turned to emotional-trigger research.

It's Not the Money Stupid!

Although management was correct that commercial/industrial customers were angry, previous findings oversimplified and distorted the issue of rate increases. These findings identified "reasonable rates" as a key driver, for which the utility was rated poorly. But none of these reports tapped into what customers meant by "reasonable rates" or their actual thought process. Instead, the findings were based on the presumption that rate increases were viewed unilaterally. In other words, anything that cost more money was unacceptable. Because the utility didn't have the independent authority to raise or lower rates, management was left feeling both helpless *and* vindicated. There was just one problem. The presumption was based on a flawed interpretation. It failed to expose the hidden reason behind commercial/industrial customer dissatisfaction.

Naturally, every executive interviewed would have opted for lower rates given the choice. But it was not rates per se that surfaced as their principal concern, nor was it the issue that caused such an uproar. Rather, it was the method the utility employed to raise rates that made the topic so explosive. Customers felt exploited by what they described as the unfair manner in which they were charged for random spikes in usage. This was the emotional trigger at the heart of the rate issue.

The utility maintained that customers simply did not understand how little control they really had over rate increases. Not true.

"Words like egregious, outrageous, arrogant, and unconscionable were tossed around."

Commercial/industrial customers were far more informed and pragmatic than management imagined. Everyone understood that rates were regulated, and they conceded that the utility had to use a "worst-case scenario" plan in order to guarantee all their customers' needs were met. It was not until they spoke in specific terms about how their rate increases had been determined that they became visibly agitated. Many described being saddled with a huge annual rate increase based upon a window as narrow as a one-time 15-minute usage spike. Words like egregious, outrageous, arrogant, and unconscionable were tossed around. And then things really started to heat up!

In marked contrast to previous findings, no one was particularly strident about rate increases in general terms, but there was deep resentment regarding what was considered an arbitrary and inherently unfair basis for calculating those increases. The utility was a "heavy handed" and "inflexible" monopoly. If the justification for rate increases was based on their "worse case scenario" argument, what happened when that "scenario" didn't materialize? There was no corollary plan to provide rebates if projected usage levels were not met. The ill will this methodology generated was profound and threatened to undermine any hope the utility had of building a supportive commercial/industrial customer coalition.

Unfairness and Complexity: A Dangerous Brew

Not only was the methodology for establishing rate increases a sore spot, customers railed against the pricing scheme's level of complexity, claiming it was surpassed only by the airline and telecommunications industries. No one understood exactly how the rate increases were assessed, but everyone was absolutely confident the system was unfair. Many of the utility's own employees were unable to explain the formula. They were equally unclear and contradictory when it came to how the rate increases were computed.

The company's inability to explain their actions or put forth a clear and consistent explanation had a chilling effect. Customers, already frustrated, were growing increasingly suspicious. Although a viable alternative did not yet exist, these commercial/industrial customers, pushed to their limit, vowed to find another delivery method.

The utility's rate increase based exclusively on "indiscriminate" usage spikes certainly brought their customers together, just not in the way they had hoped. Instead of establishing positive customer relationships, companies large and small started to proactively investigate their options. Some spoke of considering major capital expenditures for equipment that would enable them to limit what they purchased from the utility. Others planned to explore how their entire municipality might band together to take on the monopoly. A third group expressed interest in subsidizing entrepreneurial start-ups committed to opening up the marketplace.

What Do You Mean We're Not Responsive? We're Here, Aren't We?

Equally troubling was the contradictory feedback concerning responsiveness and being customer-oriented. The utility received high marks on being responsive to customer problems, yet was widely criticized for not being customer-oriented. But weren't they really the same thing? The company was at a loss to decipher what seemed to be another serious mixed message.

Survey after survey documented customer satisfaction with the utility's prompt response whenever service-related problems occurred. Management, proud of that achievement, proceeded to take that all too familiar but dangerous leap from what they knew to what they assumed. In the absence of genuine insight, they equated responsiveness with being customer-oriented. They used the two apparently similar measurement criteria interchangeably. Their marketing strategy positioned the utility as being customer oriented *precisely because* they responded quickly to customer problems. While the utility may have linked responsiveness with being customer-oriented, commercial/industrial customers did not. They held a decidedly different view.

Although commercial/industrial customers talked about the utility's "responsiveness," they conceded the company was quick to resolve emergency service related problems. So what? That was implicit in their "contract." They paid their bills, and the utility honored their obligation to provide a consistent quality of service. Such an arrangement fostered satisfaction, but never rose to the level of loyalty.

Building strong customer relationships required more. The utility's responsiveness to emergency service interruptions wasn't enough. To be truly customer-oriented, they had to go beyond solving the "exceptional" common problems and demonstrate a commitment to the needs of particular companies. Suddenly these mixed messages became clear. The utility was commended for the manner in which they handled their core business when emergencies occurred, but criticized for what was characterized as their indifference to the concerns and problems of individual customers. The company was faulted for being reactive, rather than proactive.

Senior executives within the commercial/industrial sector were angry. Technically, the utility was just another vendor, and they weren't used to vendors calling the shots or being indifferent to their needs. It was an upside down situation. Making matters worse, they had no immediate recourse, and they knew it. This one-sided relationship bred resentment that did not bode well for the future. Yes, the utility was great during an emergency, but that was no excuse for ignoring their day-to-day problems. Every customer had a story. Few had happy endings.

There were ongoing difficulties when a dispute occurred with the utility. Without an advocate, many customers found themselves enmeshed in red tape. Others told tales of attempting to upgrade faulty equipment or address service disruptions unique to a geographic location. The utility's mantra never changed. They were always "looking into it," but a resolution was elusive. Commercial/industrial customers said the utility operated like a corporate giant. They weren't approachable. Monopoly or not, they were still a service provider and needed to act like one.

Either You're With Us or You're Against Us

The utility's lack of responsiveness to individual company needs was a consistent trigger among commercial/industrial customers. And, within this context, the most emotionally charged topic of all was technology. Manufacturers were upgrading their plants with increasingly sophisticated, computer-controlled equipment to help them realize quality improvements, reduce payroll costs, curtail waste, and benefit from process re-engineering enhancements. But the more precise the equipment, the less tolerance there was for service interruptions. Depending upon the level of complexity involved, service fluctuations that once fell within acceptable ranges could now cost customers hundreds of thousands of dollars in damage to their equipment and lost business. Executives complained the utility had failed to keep pace with major technological advances; their equipment was no longer in sync with that of their customers. This was a serious problem that customers complained was met with nothing but platitudes and empty promises. It was also a textbook example of how, in the absence of genuine insight, the utility completely misinterpreted what commercial/industrial customers expected of a customer-oriented company.

As the case studies in this book have consistently revealed, the headline tends to distort the true story. Without benefit of interpretation, the utility accepted the fact that rate increases, in general terms, were the reason for customer dissatisfaction. On the flip side, they mistakenly congratulated themselves for being customer-oriented, because they responded quickly to emergency service problems. In both instances, they failed to uncover the crucial emotional triggers that explained why relationships with commercial/industrial customers were strained.

Emotional Trigger	What Emotional Triggers Revealed
Feelings	▫ They felt exploited by the utility's formula for charging rate increases. ▫ They felt ignored when requesting assistance with issues specific to their own company. ▫ They felt helpless and resentful that the balance of power was one sided.
Experiences	▫ They experienced lost business and damage to their equipment because of the utility's failure to keep pace with technological advances. ▫ They experienced platitudes and empty promises rather than actual help or support.
Needs	▫ They needed a "give and take" business relationship with a partner who helped solve their problems. ▫ They needed to have a meaningful "voice" that gave them some measure of control over their own situation.

The Method Is the Message

The clear message from the emotional-trigger research was that a "monopoly" dictates, but a "partner" has a team mentality. Although it was true that as a regulated industry the utility did not have complete autonomy, they still had choices. The opportunity to establish more meaningful customer relationships depended entirely on how they proceeded to navigate within the framework set by the legislature and regulatory agencies. Within that context, the utility had to position itself as a vendor dedicated to satisfying the needs of their customers, rather than as a monopoly providing a "take it or leave it" service.

Commercial/industrial customers understood the dictates that bound the utility. That's why, despite numerous findings to the contrary, they were not resistant to rate increases as such. However, they expected those increases to be based on reasonable criteria, instead of a formula that was viewed as arbitrary, inconsistent, and unfair. The solution required a three-step plan.

The utility had to re-examine their method of setting annual rate increases exclusively on short term one-time usage spikes. That meant aggregating a greater number of usage spikes and averaging them together to determine the annual rate increase, exploring a partial credit if the actual usage varied by more than 10 percent from the estimates, and switching from setting increases based upon a 12 month rolling period to a shorter time frame. Then, they had to launch an aggressive initiative to provide commercial/industrial customers with tangible and workable recommendations for achieving substantive reductions in usage spikes.

Finally, they had to implement a company-wide training program to ensure everyone within the organization who interacted with customers understood and could explain the rationale for, and process by which, rate increases were set. Additionally, they had to publish easy-to-read explanations of the charges and why they served as the basis for the commercial/industrial customer rate structure.

Communicate and Collaborate

Emotional-trigger research also provided the pivotal, but previously elusive, insights the utility needed in order to grasp the distinction commercial/industrial customers made between being "responsive" and being "customer-oriented." They finally understood it wasn't enough to resolve emergency service interruptions. That was considered a given. Dramatically improving customer relationships required something else entirely. It required maintaining an ongoing dialog with their customers to understand the challenges they encountered and collaborating with them on an ongoing basis to address those challenges.

At the top of the list was demonstrating a greater sensitivity to the disparity between the utility's antiquated system and the major technological improvements their customers were investing in. Short term, it wasn't possible to implement a system-wide upgrade. Nevertheless, the utility had to take positive steps to bridge the gap as a demonstration of goodwill. Once they acknowledged the seriousness of the problem, they could begin to solve it.

The first step was to conduct an internal evaluation to identify geographic regions with the highest instances of service fluctuations. That enabled the utility to prioritize upgrades by geographic clusters, based upon the number of manufacturers that experienced equipment malfunctions due to technology incompatibility.

They also began work to create and implement an alert system that would give companies a 60-minute warning whenever the utility had advance knowledge of a possible service fluctuation. The utility was committed to investing in the future, as resources permitted. In the meantime, providing advance warnings, whenever possible, was tangible evidence of their intention to become more customer-oriented.

At last, after years of mixed messages and false starts, the utility finally understood the story behind the headlines. Emotional-trigger research unlocked the insights that were needed to improve relationships with commercial/industrial customers.

SUMMING UP
IMPROVING CUSTOMER RELATIONSHIPS IN A MONOPOLY INDUSTRY

Situation

A large utility operating as a virtual monopoly still encountered challenges on numerous fronts. Both legislative and regulatory agencies demanded they hold down rates. Their commercial/industrial customers were investigating emerging alternative options. Profit margins were shrinking. Within this charged atmosphere, the utility recognized the importance of solidifying relationships with key commercial and industry customers in order to gain their support for pending legislation amid mounting public pressure. But before the utility could forge stronger relationships with this sector, they needed to clarify what appeared to be mixed customer messages. Previous survey results suggested their biggest problem was anger over recent rate hikes. This same survey, however, also included contradictory scores relative to service and responsiveness. Recognizing the need to understand what customers really meant before they could respond appropriately, the utility turned to emotional-trigger research for answers.

Commercial/Industrial Customers' Emotional Triggers

Manufacturers were outraged by what they described as an arbitrary basis for raising their rates, not the rate increases per se. They were angry and felt cheated by a formula that locked in annual charges based on narrow usage "spikes" rather than the norm. And they were equally upset by the utility's lack of responsiveness to technological advances. Commercial/industrial customers felt defenseless to protect their equipment when the utility's outmoded systems caused their own more sophisticated technology to malfunction.

Genuine Insight

Everyone understood rates were regulated. It was the practice of assessing an annual rate increase based on a particularly narrow window that generated so much ill will. Further, while the utility earned high marks for responding to emergencies, customers did not equate that with good service. Responding to emergencies resulted in customer satisfaction, but sensitivity to their particular business needs on a day-to-day basis is what fostered loyalty and built relationships.

Solution

The utility had to position itself as a vendor dedicated to satisfying customers, rather than as a monopoly providing a "take it or leave it" service. That meant aligning their priorities with those of their key customers, beginning with the "usage window" to assess annual rates. Then system upgrades had to be clustered geographically based on the number of manufacturers experiencing equipment malfunctions due to technology incompatibility.

Part V

Integrating Emotional Logic

Chapter 16

Challenges Around Every Corner

Dissecting and Managing Diverse Organizational Issues

Over the span of our careers, we all interface with individuals in a multitude of roles including those of customer, vendor, service provider, employee, management, strategic partner, investor, and perhaps even analyst. But whatever the roles assumed by the people we hope to influence, as the case studies in this book have proven, all people are emotional beings.

> The difference between hearing and really listening can be as different as night and day. And in a business environment, not listening effectively to customers, employees, and peers can mean the difference between success and failure.
> —Ken Johnson

Although we've focused exclusively on sales and marketing challenges up to this point, the applications for emotional-trigger research are unlimited. Regardless of the complex issues confronting your company, this technique will expose the emotional triggers such issues arouse and serve as the basis for crafting a response. Each organization grapples with its own unique situation, but every organization shares a common need to prosper. Although circumstances

223

vary, the common need to effectively address pressing business challenges is universally dependent upon a combination of nuanced insights and the right strategic solution.

In this chapter, we'll turn our attention to four examples of how emotional-trigger research benefited companies seeking to:

1. Restore employee morale.
2. Enhance customer communications.
3. Strengthen vendor relationships.
4. Understand analyst expectations.

1. Restoring Employee Morale: A Promising Merger Gone Awry

Mergers usually begin with high hopes. Sadly, the reality often falls short of expectations. That was the case when two multi-billion dollar companies merged their global operations. Millions were spent to launch the new enterprise. Customers were promised enhanced services, greater efficiencies, reduced costs, and more rapid turnaround times. Although these promises were being made, the company quietly scrambled behind the scenes to integrate two very different organizations. Employees were relocated from around the world to one consolidated regional operation. Inevitable disruptions occurred, but management's primary focus remained on the external marketplace. Internal concerns were secondary to addressing customer needs.

As a consequence, too many public assurances were made before measures had been taken to guarantee these assurances could be honored. Soon, the company found itself swamped with one problem after another. Statements went out to customers incorrectly. Subsequent payments were applied to the wrong accounts. Tens of millions of dollars became trapped in a bureaucratic logjam. Rather than experiencing the anticipated efficiencies of scale, front line employees were devoting the majority of their day to correcting—or trying to correct—accounting discrepancies. They were inundated with problems they didn't have the power to fix.

Morale plummeted. Turnover skyrocketed. New recruits hired to replace more seasoned employees were enmeshed in an atmosphere of frustration and inefficiency. All the while, millions and millions of dollars caught in accounting limbo continued to mount. Eventually the internal confusion could no longer be contained. As it began spilling over into the customer experience, the spate of grievances was putting long-term client relationships at risk. Faced with the loss of talented personnel, disgruntled customers, and unhappy employees, management turned to emotional-trigger research to understand the scope of the problems and what they had to do to solve them.

Emotional-trigger research revealed how management had completely misread the needs and perceptions of rank and file employees. The CEO had relied on one major communications blitz to announce the merger and detail all the associated benefits employees would realize. Pleased with the initial response, management turned their attention back to customer issues and assumed all the organizational pieces would naturally fall into place, ensuring the company's success.

That never happened. Instead, employee enthusiasm was quickly replaced by feelings of resentment. Management failed to appreciate the extent to which front-line personnel felt they had been "hung out to dry." Following

> **"Management failed to appreciate the extent to which front line personnel felt they had been 'hung out to dry.'"**

ing the major communications launch, little attention was paid to the nuts-and-bolts details required for a smooth transition. Decisions had been made at the macro level without the input of associates charged with the actual implementation of those decisions. Senior executives, continually in the loop by virtue of their positions, forgot how little had been told to employees further down in the organization.

Front-line employees had never been given the tools they needed to perform their jobs, nor the information they needed to satisfy customers. They were demoralized by the lack of advance planning that had left them on their own to cope within the newly merged organization. Under enormous pressure to perform without an adequate support system in place, huge sums of money were incorrectly applied to thousands of major accounts. The lack of systems integration was a nightmare. Employees were overwhelmed by the sheer magnitude of the task ahead. Stress levels escalated daily as the number of accounting errors grew.

Employees realized some glitches and missteps were a normal part of any merger. That wasn't what demoralized them. What demoralized them was the disregard for their needs and concerns that typified how the merger was handled. Neglecting to anticipate the need for aligning processes, procedures, and systems before the new company was "taken to market" was, in their words, inexcusable. Not only were they denied crucial systems support, but, through no fault of their own, and with no power to change the status quo, they became the brunt of customer anger. That's why so many employees quit while others simply went through the motions.

Once emotional-trigger research exposed the extent to which employees had become alienated, a task force was quickly established to identify all the systems and operational problems. The task force reviewed the findings with senior management and prioritized a punch list. A separate team was then assigned to tackle each of the high priority problems and report on their progress weekly. Every department was required to conduct a weekly staff meeting to keep all employees in the loop. Notes of the meetings went to top management, who in turn acted on key issues and communicated back throughout the company, so employees would know they'd been heard and how their issues were being handled. In order to resolve key human-resource issues, outside professionals were retained to reconcile and explain benefits, prepare job descriptions, and conduct training programs. Finally, to say thank you and inject a renewed spirit of camaraderie into the organization, management threw a fabulous party that helped restore morale.

Emotional-trigger research crystallized an important lesson: companies don't succeed unless their employees want them to! By saddling employees who formed the nucleus of the organization with all of the frustration, but none of the benefits, associated with the merger, management had nearly sabotaged their own success.

Recapping Story #1	
The Management's Perception	The initial communications launch had motivated employees and ensured that subsequent organizational issues would naturally fall into place.
The Employees' Emotional Triggers	They had been "hung out to dry." They were left to cope with angry customers with neither the tools nor the information they needed to do their job. Management had saddled front-line associates with all of the frustrations associated with the merger while they reserved the benefits for themselves.

2. Enhancing Customer Communications: The Y2K Scare

At the end of the 20th century, the world was gripped by a scare known as Y2K. It was believed this calendar problem, the coming of the year 2000, posed a looming technological disaster to computer systems, threatening grave financial and infrastructure damage that could take years to repair. Hundreds of billions of dollars were at stake. Obscure speculations on the fringes of the information technology (IT) community seemed to swell overnight into a massive flood of concern, even panic. Would the world's technology infrastructure shudder to a halt as millions of internal clocks failed to roll over to the year 2000? Would airplanes fall from the sky, automobile engines freeze, elevators lock between floors? Cooler heads eventually prevailed but a very real, very stubborn, very massive, problem did remain. The IT systems of millions of businesses weren't equipped to handle the format of the new millennium's year designations. The accounting, human resources, operations, scheduling, and communications networks—the lifeblood of the world's businesses—could in fact be jeopardized. The implications were staggering.

A global computer company with a brilliant record of quality and technological innovation believed they had achieved a breakthrough solution that gave customers reliable tools for dealing with any disruptions early and completely. Confident they had technologically superior products, the company launched a global communications campaign to maximize their perceived advantage. Yet despite all their efforts, customers seemed lukewarm, even skeptical, about their Y2K compliance program. The computer company was concerned by the underwhelming reaction to their initiatives. Seeing customer satisfaction slipping and opportunities missed, they wanted a communications strategy that would educate customers, service providers, and the media on the advantages of their solution. Time was of the essence. A rock solid understanding was needed of the specific messages that would neutralize customer fears and, more importantly, create brand confidence to increase sales. In search of direction, management turned to emotional-trigger research. Information technology directors and Y2K coordinators across a wide range of industry sectors throughout the United States and Great Britain were interviewed. The findings were dramatic and troubling. Although the computer company firmly believed that its technology solution, verification processes, and product guarantees led the industry in meeting their customers' needs, emotional-trigger research uncovered a very different state of affairs.

In stark contrast to the computer company's "inside out view," customers felt driven by factors outside their control. Barraged by shrill warnings from Y2K consultants and the media, they were frightened, angry, and discouraged. They felt the IT industry wasn't taking their concerns seriously enough. They criticized the computer company for looking at only half of the problem, leaving them to their own devices to resolve the remaining challenges. IT experts **"They criticized the computer company for only looking at half the problem, leaving them to their own devices to resolve the remaining challenges."** said business as usual wasn't enough. They were in a crisis situation, or so it seemed at the time. Year 2000 compliance was a gateway issue affecting the future of their companies. The "crisis" demanded strictly defined standards and compliance assurances. They weren't getting that. Instead, the computer company was posting lists of Y2K-compliant products and technical specifications, telling customers this would address their issues, but customers thought the lists were unreliable. Many products weren't included. Others, once listed, might disappear or later be revised without notification. IT directors questioned the benefit of replacing a defective product under warranty if fundamental operational problems could put them out of business.

Customers wanted dependable technology partners with whom they could collaborate to solve potential business-infrastructure problems of a historic scale. Far from experiencing a level of comfort and sense of partnership with the company, IT directors were anxious, dissatisfied, and even angry. As a result, brand loyalty that previously existed was being lost because IT directors believed the computer company was resistant to new information, slow to respond, and ill-informed about the real issues that concerned them most. This growing resentment negatively impacted purchase decisions. Even more ominously, customers were thinking aggressively about legal options should their systems malfunction, something the computer company had not addressed. Their customers wanted absolute guarantees. And, if the turn of the clock created an infrastructure failure, they would be looking for substantial punitive damages.

Emotional-trigger research pinpointed how the computer company's communication plan had failed and provided the blueprint for a new strategy of integrated initiatives. Corporate messages were rewritten to emphasize the comprehensive nature of the support provided. These messages became part of a worldwide effort to introduce customers, dealers, and the press to the company's innovative solutions. At the same time, the computer company began a proactive policy of partnership with customers. Equipped with new insights into the most pressing Y2K legal and operational issues, they provided information and procedures that dealt with their customers' most serious concerns.

Together, strong message development, redirecting the focus of reseller support, establishing partnerships with major accounts, introducing protections from future legal liability, promoting the company's exceptional technology expertise, identifying solutions for key customer issues, and rolling out a comprehensive awareness drive, positioned the computer company as the Y2K-industry leader. Once they successfully regained their customers' loyalty, they dramatically exceeded sales goals for their proprietary solutions.

Recapping Story #2

The Computer Company's Perception	They had achieved a breakthrough solution that gave customers reliable tools for dealing with any potential Y2K disruptions early and completely. Their communications program introducing these proprietary solutions would be enthusiastically embraced by customers.
The Customers' Emotional Triggers	They were left without a reliable technology partner to collaborate with on all aspects of the Y2K challenge. Instead, the computer company provided only partial remedies and tried to superimpose their solutions, rather than seeking to understand the issues that most concerned their customers.

3. Strengthening Vendor Relationships: Supply Chain Disruptions

A major national retailer, historically the leader in their category, was struggling to overcome declining sales in the face of internal setbacks and their strongest competitor's rapid climb. Stores and warehouses were clogged with excess inventory. Strapped for cash, funds to purchase new merchandise were limited. Desperate to jumpstart sales, management applied increasing pressure on their vendors in order to squeeze out every possible concession. The situation was growing more precarious by the day.

Nevertheless, management was confident they had the upper hand. **"...management was confident they had the upper hand."** A rash of industry consolidations had left many suppliers at the mercy of fewer, but more powerful, masters. Newly consolidated retail chains exacerbated a tenuous situation by exerting increased pressure on suppliers to lower their prices. As the retailer's fortunes dwindled, some vendors had already gone out of business, while others had been forced to file for bankruptcy.

Many vendors needed this account to survive and went to considerable lengths to be supportive, but even they had limits. Faced with diminishing sales, late payments, punitive charges, and arbitrary add-on fees, several suppliers finally had enough. Spending more money than ever chasing after a shrinking account, their efforts were rewarded with new demands and larger financial penalties. In desperation, a number of vendors pulled the plug and stopped shipping merchandise. The threat of a supply-chain disruption had suddenly morphed into a full blown crisis. Without an uninterrupted flow of goods, the retailer had little chance of survival. At last, an already lopsided relationship crossed the line. Ongoing capitulation on financial matters had seriously eroded many manufacturers' profits. Excessive demands accompanied by promises of additional business in the near future were no longer credible. Vendors felt abused.

Punitive charges assessed for non-compliance with purchase-order agreements topped the manufacturers' list of grievances. These were especially galling, because, in most cases, the charges were arbitrary, unfair, or simply wrong. Suppliers were riled by management's tactics, and their failure to address systemic problems that were at the root of compliance discrepancies. Vendors complained that countless problems occurred at both the front and back end of most transactions.

At the front end, vendors were maddened by the company's flawed forecasting system that caused ongoing manufacturing and shipping complications. Referred to as a purchase projection, suppliers were expected to reserve manufacturing time and lock in production orders on the basis of these projections, but management wouldn't commit to purchasing the quantities manufacturers were told to produce and reserve. Although widespread inaccuracies ensued, suppliers were expected to absorb all the costs. The retailer made the mistakes, the vendors paid for them. It was an impossible situation.

At the back end, the retailer's compliance program specified when merchandise was to be delivered and set the minimum percentage of an order that had to be filled. If the terms were not met, vendors were penalized. Manufacturers agreed they should be held accountable for their commitments but were outraged over how the program was administered and considered it a form of extortion. It was a powder keg that had finally exploded. Shortcomings with the retailer's distribution system caused most of the problems. For example, if an order was split on multiple trucks, the percentage of the order filled was based solely on the first truck, resulting in suppliers being assessed a fee. If a shipment utilized multiple delivery methods, only one method was counted and, once again, vendors were fined. Or, if the manufacturer's trucks arrived at the specified time, but the retailer was unable to unload them, they were also charged a late fee.

Even when suppliers had the proper documentation it took months to resolve discrepancies. Worse still, the retailer benefited from the float on their money for months at a time, while the charges remained in dispute. Vendors already saddled with declining sales had to digest significant administrative expense just to document the retailer's mistakes. These charges were seen as a thinly veiled subsidy to insulate management from their own self-inflicted problems. Manufacturers felt cheated out of their money.

Before vendor relationships could be strengthened and shipments resumed, management had to demonstrate a sincere desire to change the way they operated. The situation demanded a sweeping goodwill gesture. Because nothing would garner as much goodwill as the immediate suspension of the existing compliance program, that's what management did. They conceded the current program was inequitable and promised to fix existing problems before imposing any further penalties. Vendors were thrilled. They never expected such swift and decisive action. This tangible evidence of change laid the foundation for the beginning of a genuine partnership, one that was mutually beneficial.

Emotional-trigger research revealed how powerless suppliers felt to affect the decisions that impacted their own companies and how mistreated they felt by the retailer. These insights led to a series of new initiatives designed to reverse course and reopen the supply chain. Systems and logistical operations between manufacturers and the retailer were aligned for compatibility. Discipline-to-discipline planning sessions led to improved coordination, enhanced efficiencies, and fewer compliance discrepancies. A vendor advisory panel was formed to address shared concerns. The efforts paid off. The company was praised for admitting their mistakes and listening to vendor concerns. Within a year, management won the trust of suppliers, who applauded the integrity and respect with which they were now being treated. Although vendors recognized the company still wrestled with many challenges, a real breakthrough had occurred. Manufacturers no long felt alienated. Confident that punitive measures were a thing of the past, previously disenfranchised suppliers resumed normal shipments.

Recapping Story #3	
The Retail Management's Perception	They had the upper hand. Vendors couldn't afford to lose their business.
The Vendors' Emotional Triggers	Management had pushed them to their limit. It was one thing to negotiate tough minded concessions, but punitive charges crossed the line. They felt cheated and exploited.

4. Understanding Analyst Expectations: A Growth Company's Underperforming Stock

Organizations seeking to raise capital or put their company up for sale are particularly fixated on the need to demonstrate stock appreciation. Facing such circumstances, many executives battling depressed stock valuations that seem at odds with market fundamentals have struggled to overcome the resistance of influential analysts. Sometimes, analysts hesitant to recommend a stock articulate clear-cut reasons. At other times, their reasons are an enigma. When those reasons are based on gut feelings, they may be less forthright or willing to confront management directly. That was the case with an entrepreneurial start-up that skyrocketed to become a leading provider of security software with a decade.

Recognized internationally as one of the top in their industry, the company's sales were soaring. Their award-winning applications were distributed worldwide. New product introductions were consistently well received, and the customer base was expanding rapidly. Accomplishments aside, the stock price remained unchanged. Management turned to emotional-trigger research to find out why analysts refused to award them a "buy" recommendation.

Analysts readily acknowledged the demand for the company's high-quality products. But they had gnawing reservations about top management and were uncomfortable sharing their personal reservations with them face-to-face. Similar to so many start-ups that are the brainchild of a brilliant visionary, that same visionary was now running the entire operation. Analysts were concerned by the dearth of business experience, management expertise, and real world pragmatism. They felt the organization, staffed with and headed by technology wizards full of enthusiasm but short on maturity and discipline, actually threatened the company's long-term prospects. To them, it was a high-risk proposition. After the dot-com bubble burst a few years earlier, hundreds of analysts lost their jobs. The experience left survivors chastened. They were more cautious than before and less willing to go out on a limb.

The company's reputation for customer service was viewed as a two-edged sword. Analysts worried that new products, created to meet specific market needs, were mismanaged. They referenced numerous instances when customers called to say they liked a particular product and went on to inquire about the possibility of a customized enhancement. The tech staff was always accommodating. Their standard response was "No problem. We can do that for you." Then they proceeded to make a "one off" enhancement for that client only. The enhancements were never incorporated in the overall product specifications, nor was the marketplace made aware the enhancements even existed. Consequently, the company was the big loser. Failure to leverage these product improvements resulted in the loss of all the incremental revenue such improvements would generate. Worse still, the company ended up with products that had different value to different customers. By happenstance the company had inadvertently created a second, customized business model that wasn't sustainable. In spite of the organization's impressive sales growth, the absence of professional leadership or operational efficiencies made analysts very uneasy about recommending the company. Yet rather than confronting management directly, they skirted sensitive personnel

> **"By happenstance, the company had inadvertently created a second, customized business model that wasn't sustainable."**

concerns choosing to take a more passive approach. They simply declined to rate the stock as a "buy."

Once the emotional triggers that prevented analysts from supporting the stock were uncovered, management realized they had been operating against their own interests. Eager to position the company for a lucrative sale, they took decisive action. A new CEO with proven business credentials was hired to run the organization. Operational efficiencies were put in place to ensure product enhancements were properly managed. Although innovation remained the organization's hallmark, measures were implemented to leverage revenue opportunities. Slowly the analysts took notice. Their recommendations became bullish. Within a few years, the stock had risen to a level consistent with the company's sales growth. Within five years, the company was sold for several hundred million dollars.

Recapping Story #4	
The Management's Perception	The company's security software products were well received and sales were soaring. There was no justification for analysts to refrain from rating their stock as a "buy."
The Analysts' Emotional Triggers	The company was run by young technology wizards who exhibited neither maturity nor discipline. Their lack of experience and management expertise jeopardized the company's long term prospects. Analysts, however, were too uncomfortable to critique management when the nature of their critique was personal. Candor made them too uneasy.

Emotional-Trigger Research: Limitless Possibilities

In the Introduction we began with the assertion that customers act on emotion, and throughout this book, including the case studies presented in this chapter, we have repeatedly illustrated the truth of that assertion. In almost any business encounter, emotion, not logic, drives behavior. Whether you're interacting with customers, employees, vendors, members, donors, strategic partners, suppliers, investors, board members, or analysts, remember one thing: they're all people, and people are, have always been, and will always continue to be emotional beings. Understanding what motivates them on a visceral level provides the critical insights you'll need to solve complex problems and develop the right strategies for future success. In addition to the examples we've already shared, emotional-trigger research has proven effective at increasing memberships, framing Six Sigma initiatives, instituting process re-engineering, and restructuring internal organizations. The applications are truly limitless because, regardless of your challenge, the right solution will always depend upon your ability to establish an emotional connection with your target audience.

Chapter 17

Final Thoughts

Thriving in an Increasingly Complex World

The limitations of traditional research may have slowed or impeded a company's ability to navigate the competitive landscape in simpler times. Now, such limitations can be catastrophic in the radically shifting environment of the 21st century. Business has always been difficult and complex. It has always required listening to customers, anticipating their needs, understanding the competition, and taking all those factors into account when making strategic decisions. But today, businesses confront an entirely new world order. Global dynamics are rapidly transforming the way companies will be forced to operate in the coming years.

> We can't solve problems by using the same kind of thinking we used when we created them.
> —Albert Einstein

The world has simultaneously become both larger and smaller. There are no longer defined boundaries. Companies are no longer restricted by physical brick and mortar locations or territories that can be served by a centralized sales force. Sweeping technological advances have, quite literally, created markets without borders.

239

At the same time, the world has grown smaller. Within a nanosecond, customers in one part of the world can share experiences with others halfway across the globe. The speed and scale of these interactions can redirect entire markets. The stakes have never been higher. Understanding what really motivates an increasingly diverse and demanding customer base, one that is now clearly in the driver's seat, has never been more important, or more challenging.

What will all this mean? And what role does emotional-trigger research play in this new market paradigm? Science increasingly tells us that emotion, not rational thought, is the key to customer behavior. We know customers' strongest, most immediate motivations are reactions to impulses and feelings they often don't recognize. Logical or politically correct explanations for their actions come later, if at all. Traditional information-gathering techniques and statistically based forms of market research fail to provide a nuanced window into your customers' behavior, because they capture answers, not insights.

Announcing a New World Order

At a time when gaining such insights has never been more crucial, a single consideration trumps all other reasons for exploiting the power of emotion-oriented research. It is the radically different, shockingly new, and historically unique nature of the environment businesses must master in the 21st century. Running a successful company has always demanded a set of lightning reflexes, working together in a balancing act of analysis, adaptation, and real-time understanding of customers. Now something completely unprecedented has been added: the ability to cope with an exponential pace of disruptive change.

The implications of the scale and depth of this change are impossible to fully predict, but we can say plainly enough that it will compel businesses to adapt as rapidly as the social, economic, and technological environment in which they operate is changing. Only companies that have honed their ability to respond quickly will thrive in the coming years. Such companies will know who their customers are, what they want, how to reach them, and, most importantly, how to connect with them personally. At its core, this specific ability to connect directly, almost intuitively, with customers is the inherent power of emotional-trigger research and at the center of its growing importance.

A Landscape Like None Before

We must begin with a more in-depth look at this new environment to get a better grasp of what it means in concrete terms. The tectonic shifts impacting businesses globally including the volume of critical data, demographic swings, political upheavals, population movements, mutating work attitudes, cultural transformations, economic restructuring, off-shoring, and the explosion of new technologies, are advancing at breakneck speed. These, along with many other factors, are compounded for large multinational corporations. For small companies, the challenges can be imminent threats.

The idea of massive shifts in the business environment might seem too abstract to be of use, but they aren't merely a theoretical concept. Each of us is impacted by such shifts on a daily basis. Increasingly, businesses will find themselves marketing to customers who were born into the political, technological, and economic setting of the new world order. These customers will have always lived with computers, cell phones, paperless media, globalization, diversity, and unfocused security threats. We could list comparisons and statistics endlessly, obsolete almost before they are published, proving that changes in customer experiences and mindsets continue to accelerate.

New industrial segments that feed the global supply chain are created, and sometimes suddenly disappear, in unpredictable ways. Companies large or small can find themselves suddenly as front-page news because of a defective product produced by an anonymous supplier on another continent, or because of rude customer service in their own backyard. Social networks that never sleep grow organically, linking hundreds of millions of customers into virtual networks.

Organizations are discovering that the "level playing field" of the world market is not level. In fact, there are peaks of new opportunity that continually arise from the surrounding landscape. In record time, hot new markets give way quickly to even hotter and newer markets. Companies will be perpetually challenged to identify the next peak and get to the "summit" before their competitors.

How, in the midst of such pervasive change, do businesses find their best customers? How do they

> **"...they framed the challenge as the ability to effectively utilize marketing as a conduit to and from customers."**

identify and meet the needs of these customers? How do they successfully bring their goods and services to market? In our discussions with senior executives from around the world, they emphasized one major factor as a determinant of future success. Specifically, they framed the challenge as the ability to effectively utilize marketing as a conduit to and from customers.

Companies must grow beyond the notion of simply *selling* to customers and find ways to form a genuine connection with them, one that provides realistic insights into customer needs and motivations, while, at the same time, opening a two-way channel of communication, one that flows from customers to businesses and from businesses back to their customers.

Redefining Value: The Same Only Different

At the highest level, much of the challenge in shifting business models comes from the fact that goods, services, and information can be produced, distributed, accepted, or rejected quickly and cheaply. Rapidly evolving communications platforms, manufacturing methods, global labor transfers, and free markets are making this possible.

Almost anything businesses provide is part of this free flowing global network. One of the cardinal features of the new world economy is that the price of manufacture or distribution is often near or effectively at zero. The ingredients in pharmaceuticals and cosmetics, for example, cost pennies. Music and video disks can be manufactured for under a dollar. News reports and market analyses costing thousands of dollars to create can be circulated indefinitely. Increasingly, there is little correlation between actual cost and inherent value.

So why would customers pay a premium for some goods or services? Because when customers buy a market report, they are not buying the paper it is printed on. They are buying the expertise of those who produced it. They are buying assurance, the assurance that the content is as reliable as possible before they act on it. Why would customers pay a premium for a particular drug, one that might even cost thousands of dollars per dose, when the chemicals it contains represent a fraction of the pharmaceutical's price? The purchase decision is based on trust, trust in the doctors, pharmacists, researchers, and manufacturers who attest to a medication's effectiveness and safety before they use it. Why would customers pay retail for a music CD or film on DVD they could copy for free? They are buying a superior experience. They are buying personal satisfaction, because they derive enjoyment knowing their recording is complete, of optimum quality, and the authentic work of people they admire. And while customers shop for the best prices on air travel, they rely on reputable sellers that are household names. Why? Because they want to feel confident their tickets will be honored. They need a guarantee of reliability before they commit to a vital service.

What Will Success Demand?

The common thread in these examples, and many others we could name, emerges when we take the objective view—the customer's view. In a swirl of falling prices, commoditization, counterfeiting, and free information, what can your company offer customers that is not easily imitated, copied, or falsified? They will tell you if you know the right questions to ask, and ask them in the right way. All forms of value share a common secret. They have to be unlocked. Not just in real time, but, more importantly, prior to the fact. Organizations will need to identify, with great precision, the opportunities for convergence between what they can genuinely deliver in a differentiated and superior way with the most authentic needs, frustrations, and demands of their customers. Unlocking these insights is the intrinsic value of emotional-trigger research.

As our case studies revealed, our clients often believed they were supplying value and couldn't understand why their customers weren't responding. They failed to recognize how their own frustrations and assumptions, often accepted as gospel, may have led to a misunderstanding of their customers' needs. They did not immediately appreciate how the revolutionary waves of change, sweeping through industries and markets, will involve new kinds of understanding and new skill sets, that the "tried and true" approaches they used to confront business challenges had become obsolete.

Customer Power

As we work with clients to help them develop or reinvent their sales and marketing strategies, we have seen them increasingly challenged by these dramatic shifts. Most are mature, sophisticated companies, with well informed, progressive management. But the trends businesses confront have no real precedent in their scale, complexity, or speed. The new world we have entered requires new ways of seeing, new ways of thinking, a new understanding of opportunities, just to stay in the race. Success requires fresh approaches to imagination and innovation.

One of the defining realities of the 21st century is that customers play a profoundly different and more influential role than at any time in history. Better educated and more discerning, they have access to vast amounts of information about products, services, prices, competitive alternatives, quality, and most other aspects of a purchase decision. In short, as customers exert increasing control, businesses must be prepared to continuously anticipate and monitor their expectations. The ubiquitous availability of information means that concerns, demands, perceptions, and behavior can be shared among customers outside the control of management. Transparent, immediate, positive responses are the only choices possible in such an environment.

What we show our clients, and hope we have also shown you, is how an understanding of emotional-trigger research offers your organization a revolutionary method to identify what motivates your customers to buy. In a constantly fluid business environment, the value of having the most intimate knowledge of your customer's true motivations cannot be overstated.

Emotional Insights: The New Currency

Companies that struggled to adapt to the 20th century will likely find the 21st century impossible for them. These organizations continue to rely on statistically quantifiable data that may produce factual, but nevertheless unclear, misleading, or only partial answers. Perhaps these same organizations opt to depend upon flawed and generally discredited, qualitative research methods such as focus groups or structured in-depth interviews. Either way, they are bent on stockpiling information, rather than digging for nuggets of emotional insight. Yes, it's possible to digitize information. It can be stored on databases. It can be sliced and diced in unlimited mutations. But information is not the same as insight, and it never will be.

Relying on insights offers businesses a more effective way to increase customer sales in complex and uncertain times. Technology aside, uncovering emotional insights is the domain of humans. Information alone fails to provide a comprehensive picture of your customer as a person, though that is how your customers want to be perceived and treated. Gaining such a perspective is beyond what quantitative research or structured surveys are capable of achieving.

"Information alone fails to provide a comprehensive picture of your customer as a person, though that is how your customers want to be perceived and treated."

Conceding the point will not be enough. Many organizations may still fail to uncover crucial customer insights. There are several possible explanations. The most likely is that companies begin a research initiative with a set of beliefs, essentially predictions, based on a pre-existing internal hypothesis. The testing and evaluation that follows starts in the middle, not the beginning, of the marketing process. Almost by design, researchers set out to reinforce preliminary assumptions by determining whether the initial hypothesis resonates with customers. Such a conventional approach asks "How can we sell more of our product or service?" But that's the wrong question. The primary question should be "What product or service does my customer want or need?"

The 21st century will be the century of the customer. To repeat what we said at the very beginning of this book, more than ever, companies must accept that the motivations customers act on are seldom logical, predictable, or even conscious. Instead, their strongest responses stem from one source: emotion. It really is a deceptively simple reality that permanently changes how successful businesses must go about understanding their customers and what motivates them to buy. Facts and statistics are one dimensional. Conversely, emotional trigger insights are penetrating and nuanced. They reveal opportunities and suggest strategic solutions that were not immediately obvious.

As we bring together lessons learned from companies that achieved market success using emotional-trigger research, we see how this creative and highly adaptable problem solving technique has helped organizations understand, connect with, and act on the emotions that drive their customers' decisions. We see how research and analysis that elicits the often unconscious motivations customers act upon can be a tool as powerful and paradigm-shifting as the business landscape in which we find ourselves. Emotional-trigger research digs below the superficiality of what people say to the far deeper level of hearing what they really mean. It demonstrates how to reach beyond the obvious and capitalize on the unexpected. Such insights have empowered businesses across this country, and throughout the world, to respond to their customers' emotional triggers in more intimate, powerful, and ultimately successful ways than traditional marketing techniques can hope to achieve in the tumultuous marketplace of the 21st century.

Index

About the Authors

Linda Goodman   Michelle Helin

Linda Goodman and Michelle Helin are independent business consultants who have served as senior sales and marketing officers in the hospitality, entertainment and retail sectors. Linda has been a member of the Executive Committee of divisions of Federated Department Stores, Midland Bank of England, Cole National, and The Body Shop. Michelle has been a member of the Board of Directors of Thomas Cook, Senior Vice President of Marketing for SAM's Warehouse Club, and served on the operating committees for Texas Air subsidiaries SystemOne, Inc., and Continental and Eastern sales. They met at American Broadcasting Company where Michelle served as Vice President of Special Projects and Linda was the Corporate General Manager of new business development for the Radio Division.

Both Linda and Michelle have had a lifetime interest in understanding what motivates human behavior and, after leaving the corporate world, it was a natural next step to leverage their interest and experience in this arena to assist companies in developing and leveraging this critical insight to create winning strategies.

They have led seminars, developed workshops, and given speeches on a variety of sales and marketing topics for both companies and professional organizations including The American Marketing Association, The Direct Marketing Association, The International Association of Business Communicators, The Houston Business Forum, and The Executive Council, a worldwide network of CEOs. They have worked extensively with Angel Networks, Developing Technology Centers, and have been guest lecturers at Smith College, Pepperdine University, and Rice University.

Linda is based in Avon, Connecticut and Michelle is headquartered in Houston, Texas. Their clients, located in the United States and around the world, have come from diverse industries ranging from Fortune 100 corporations to entrepreneurial start-ups. A representative sampling includes: Kodak, Schlumberger LTD, SAM's Warehouse Club, multiple divisions of Omnicom Group Inc., KPMG, CyrusOne, AT&T Lucent Technology, Compaq Computer Corporation, Disney Corporation, General Electric Corporation, Leisure Concepts Management, and Tribe Pictures.

For more information, visit *www.emotionaltriggerresearch.com.*